Praise for Gary Schne

"I've worked with Gary for more than a _____, _____ _____ _____ _____
top PR pros in the business. He always delivers guests with something
my viewers and listeners need to hear. As a former journalist, he
understands the needs of those of us in the media for timely, topical
voices. When he pitches you, pay attention."

SEAN HANNITY, *Fox News Channel and syndicated*
radio host

"ROAR has patiently coached me through a process to get my message
out in ways that shine with my passion, resonate with my diverse
audiences and move them to action."

JESSICA STOLLINGS, *Speaker, author, blogger*
and President, ReGenerations

"Gary Schneeberger is a consummate professional in public relations
and crisis management. I've had the opportunity to observe him in
numerous settings and admire that he gets things done—competently,
compassionately and creatively."

MIKE HUCKABEE, *Former Arkansas governor,*
TV talk-show host and presidential candidate

Praise for BITE THE DOG

"Gary's experience as both a journalist and public-relations executive
highlighted on these pages gives him the perfect perspective to help
you shape your message and ensure it impacts others."

ROMA DOWNEY, *Emmy-nominated actress and*
producer, Touched by an Angel, The Bible

"As a public–relations executive, Gary possesses that intangible quality—an ability to identify an opportunity as well as craft and communicate a message in a compelling and captivating manner. He is passionate and throws his heart and soul into every project he manages. So it should come as no surprise that in the writing of *Bite the Dog*, he's turned his blood into ink, delivering both a practical manual for PR as well as a wildly entertaining personal memoir."

JIM DALY, President, Focus on the Family

"Whether you are a seasoned communicator or a newbie on the scene, *Bite the Dog* is a must-read. In his thoughtful and witty way, Gary has effectively explained and modeled the time-tested importance of the art of effective public relations. The value of his expert coaching on being the most effective you can be is incalculable."

THE HONORABLE MARY BONO, Principal at Faegre Baker Daniels Consulting, former U.S. Representative, California

"Within weeks of my starting to work with Gary, he had leveraged events and opportunities to give me a greater platform for my message. *Bite the Dog* offers more than principles to ponder; it provides disciplines to practice that will help you use the media to reach more people than you thought possible."

BRAD KULLMAN, speaker and author, Losing to Win: How Incentivized Losing Undermines the Integrity of Our Major Professional Sports Leagues *and* Hardwired for Life: Human Understanding Beyond Surface Personality

"Earned media is the brass ring of marketing goals — yet powerful public relations remains a mystery even to those of us who live and breathe branding and marketing. Gary demystifies the path to achieving the earned media that smart brand leaders crave, but are often at a loss to realize. With *Bite the Dog*, Gary puts the power of PR in everyman's hands. And he does it in true Gary style: smart, clear, cogent, actionable and always thoroughly entertaining."

CHERYL FARR, *Founder & Chief Brand Officer, SIGNAL.csk Brand Partners*

"Many of us want to make an impact and don't know how without being obnoxious or paying a fortune for a 'pro.' This book, written by a pro, is a glimpse into helpful and at times hilarious advice that is applicable to all. I've known and worked with Gary for more than a decade, and he practices what he preaches here. This book will help you focus your vision, refine your goals and craft and create opportunities for your message to reach the media and the masses."

ELISHA KRAUSS, *DailyWire.com*

"I've had the misfortune of engaging in PR battles with Gary Schneeberger, and I can tell you it is no fun. Gary is simply the best in the business and a true PR guru. *Bite the Dog* offers his keen insights and lets you in on the secrets of his success. This is a must-read book for anyone who wants to learn about the art of public relations."

WAYNE BESEN, *Communications Director, Open the Government*

"As a journalist, I have always loved working with Gary because he understands the power of relationships when it comes to getting a great story told and shared. He recognizes the creator of the universe is also the creator of public relations, and it's with this heart he offers a blueprint for how he's become the best at what he does."

EFREM GRAHAM, *Host, Studio 5, CBN*

BITE THE DOG

BUILD A *PR* STRATEGY TO MAKE *NEWS* THAT *MATTERS*

February 2021

Ransom —

Always remember, if you want to BITE THE DOG, you cannot Let It Be! :) I hope you find I'm speaking words of wisdom on these pages...

[signature]

BITE THE DOG

BUILD A PR STRATEGY TO MAKE NEWS THAT MATTERS

GARY SCHNEEBERGER

Niche Pressworks
Indianapolis

Dedication

For

Kelly, the rose of my heart

Alyssa and Hunter, the petals

&

Heather, the first blossom

Acknowledgements

I've remarked often during my career how fortunate I am to have collected so many memorable and meaningful experiences over what is now the last 30-plus years. The cool thing about writing a book that draws from those experiences is that it really gets you thinking about the memorable people and meaningful relationships that made any of it possible.

My list starts with a literal handful of individuals—five fingers' worth—who fostered my love of writing and bolstered my practice of it. They made everything in my professional life as a communicator possible.

My big sister, Jill Sprague, who taught me how to write—as in how to form letters and build them into words. It birthed in me the joy of arranging those words into sentences—beginning with my first story, *The Pig*, written in kindergarten and still lurking in a file cabinet, embarrassing phonetic misspellings and all. I love you, Sis. Thank you for investing time and care in your annoying little brother.

My mom, the late Martha "Marty" Johnson, who rewarded my fascination with words by buying me an electric typewriter when I was barely into double digits. That machine was my passageway to a new world of creation and imagination, Ma, and I know it was not easy for a single parent to make that trip possible. How I love and miss you.

The late John Niemeier, my ninth-grade social studies teacher, who took the time to write notes encouraging me to keep developing what he saw as my natural gifts as a writer. He told me once that an assignment was "one of the best I have ever received from the over 2,000 students I have taught in the last 16 years. I like your creative style of writing." Thank you, Mr. N., for being generous with that all-important first affirmation from someone who had a different last name than I did.

Frank Carmichael, editor and publisher of *Happenings* magazine in my hometown of Kenosha, Wisconsin, who in 1983 took a chance on an 18-year-old college kid and gave him his first paying writing gig—as his TV critic, teaching me to write for the people and not my professors. It has been an honor, Frank, to come full circle now that I've returned home after 29 years and serve you as a ROAR client.

And the late Jim Bishop, the Pulitzer-Prize winning journalist who mentored me in the newsroom like a father mentors a son in the home. This is how I described what he taught me when I had the honor of eulogizing him in 2013: "What Jim knew as a reporter and what Jim taught as an editor was that journalism was not about reporting *news events*; it was discovering and sharing *news stories*. He pushed you, he trained you, to look for the story beneath the facts. To keep rooting around till you found something to show, rather than just something to tell." Thanks for always being there, Doc.

On the professional front, thanks and gratitude to Gary Metro, the veteran cops-and-courts reporter who taught me as an untrained cops-and-courts reporter that objectivity was impossible, but fairness was mandatory; Kevin Kraft and Carroll Wilson, my first and last great editors, who poured their best journalism and leadership into me, and made me better at both; Jim Daly, president and chief voice and face of Focus on the Family, for turning me loose to help make him a household name and setting the finest example of servant leadership I've ever been privileged to serve; Nicole Gebhardt, my publisher, who coached and cared for me as I conquered the learning curve of adapting more than three decades of writing for a living to a discipline whose difficulty I vastly underestimated; and to the scores of men and women who have called me "boss" at the many stops along my path, who have honored me with their commitment to growing while stretching me in the process.

And to all the reporters, editors, hosts, producers, commentators and journalism executives to whom I've pitched stories and appearances through the years, thank you whether you said "yes" or "no." In the former instance, you loaned your megaphone to a client who was able to speak his, her or its heart to your audience. In the latter instance, you pushed me to new and better ways to craft pitches that bite the dog.

On the personal front, my love always, in all ways, to my wife, Kelly, who gave me a second chance at once in a lifetime and composed with me our own man-bites-dog love story; my appreciation to Jim Neibaur, my friend and brother since college, a prolific author who has often acknowledged me in his books even when I didn't do anything to deserve it, who did something to deserve his mention here by never letting up on encouraging me to write one; gratitude for kindnesses that can never be repaid to Karla Dial, Marcus Osburn, Brian Cragin and Tom Hovsepian, who guided me to the most important decision of my life and stabilized me after I made it; and a hug and/or handshake to the scores of men and women who have called me "friend" at the many stops along my path, who honored me with their easy laughter and, when necessary, hard truth. Please know that I and my life are richer for knowing you.

Last in these acknowledgements, and I pray nowhere else, I pledge all that I am to Jesus Christ, my Lord and Lover of my Soul, who gave His life as a ransom for many—history's most remarkable man-bites-dog story.

Contents

PR-Verb Index

This Isn't a Book;
It's a Recipe for Secret Sauce

How do some people and causes make it into the news when others—maybe even better ones—don't seem to be able to? If you've ever wondered about the secret sauce necessary to make headlines happen, this is your book. More accurately, it's your recipe to learn how to whip up that sauce for yourself.

My friend and former colleague, Gary Schneeberger, has long helped me get a spotlight shone on the passions of my heart—be they the work I do helping foster children find forever families or convincing the local paper to report on my daughter winning her first national equestrian championship. I'll admit, I didn't always understand what motivates the press or have insight into the behind-the-scenes factors that can make or break a story. Gary's encouragement and expertise helped me take my message to places I never thought I'd reach, to make news, as the book's subtitle says, that matters.

On these pages, Gary lays out a step-by-step process in a fun and remarkably clear way that will bring many more ears and eyeballs to the insights and services you offer—all without a giant advertising budget, which most of us don't have.

As both a former reporter and editor and a PR professional extraordinaire, Gary shares 30 years of his best lessons learned to help us all better understand how to maximize the impact of what we say and do in what he calls the mediasphere—demystifying public-relations lingo like "earned media" and, well, "man bites dog."

With his characteristic flair and humor, Gary brings home his clear counsel with insider stories from Hollywood to the NFL, from CNN to Fox News—tales that will surprise, delight and equip you to magnify your voice using the media's megaphone.

If what you have to say matters, then it matters that you grab this resource and let Gary's talents advance your goals. You won't find a tastier sauce on the subject.

Kelly Rosati
President, KMR Consulting
KellyRosati.net

INTRODUCTION

Here's Where I Tell You What the Title Means

"Jim's been in a serious accident."

That's what the voice on the other end of the phone told me, shocking and serious news since Jim was my boss (and friend): Jim Daly, president of the family-help ministry Focus on the Family.

I could tell from my colleague's tone that the first, worst thing you fear from such a call wasn't true. Jim was still with us. He had been riding motorcycles with a buddy in the Rocky Mountains, near Focus' headquarters in Colorado Springs, and had wiped out on a combination of loose dirt and sharp turn, breaking his left ankle rather nastily and gashing up his left forearm. But he was in good spirits, I was told, and would probably only have to be in the hospital overnight.

Well, then, I thought as I hung up, what am I waiting for?

See, as Focus' VP of communications, I was in the midst of trying to raise Jim's public profile as the group's second-generation leader. It had been less than a year since the resignation of Dr. James Dobson, the beloved child psychologist who had taken the organization from a one-room office to the Oval Office, advising presidents, influencing public policy and helping hundreds of thousands of families over the course of 30 years. Jim was in many ways the anti-Dr. Dobson: a generation younger, not a PhD expertly doling out answers to thorny questions about marriage and parenting, but a husband and father working those issues out day-to-day just like everybody else. He'd inherited Dr. Dobson's radio show and its millions of listeners and still guided the

1

train along the same path of biblically based counsel that had always kept constituents hopping aboard. But Jim was a conductor of much different style, and the cable TV news shows and publications with seven-digit circulations that kept Dr. Dobson on speed-dial weren't calling him for interviews on news that affected families.

That was not good for me, for Jim, or for Focus on the Family.

So, I called the reporter with whom I had the best relationship at the local newspaper. I offered him details of Jim's accident before the local TV affiliates, his competition, could get wind of it from first-responder reports. I gave him tidbits no one would ever find in those reports—written since the Jurassic era of police and firefighters as lifelessly as the English language allows.

Focus on the Family President Jim Daly was back in the radio studio days after his serious motorcycle crash that landed on Page 1 of the local paper for its man-bites-dog qualities. (Personal photo.)

The story I presented in our chat was not about a CEO surviving a motorcycle accident; it was about an adventurous, vigorous guy who got hurt enjoying a slightly dangerous hobby. And now he was having a jolly time even while wracked with pain.

"Jim's a robust, active guy, a real athlete," I told the reporter, a quote he used to close out his story, which wound up on the next day's front page. "This is how he relaxes and unwinds—riding Harleys in the mountains. Not my idea of taking it easy, but that's Jim."[1]

Jim added a nice touch himself from his hospital bed, telling the reporter that his doctors had said they could see the tendons working in his arm as they sewed it up, like something out of *The Terminator*. He added with a laugh that when he flipped the bike "all I could see was sky then dirt, sky then dirt."[2]

So why did I relate such a serious story as a frolic? Why, instead of tears, had I offered laughs? Perhaps more to the point, why did my boss—the guy who could have been maimed or worse and still was staring down the barrel of eight weeks of arduous rehab—happily play along? Because Jim Daly knew that if you want the kind of media attention that advances and enhances your brand, you have to bite the dog.

A LITTLE MORE ABOUT YOU, ME AND THEM

I'm guessing you're holding this book right now because you have something you want to say that you want people to hear. Maybe you think of it as your calling. Maybe it's your job. Maybe it's a message you feel you've been uniquely equipped to share. There's a good chance it's all three. In fact, you're probably already putting that message out there—via a blog, an email list or public-speaking gigs. And yet … you feel like something's missing. You could/should have a bigger audience, bigger influence, bigger impact. You're not yet achieving your goal, at least not on the level you'd like, to change hearts with what's in your heart. You want more, most likely not just for yourself, but for those who could benefit from what you have to say, and you aren't getting it. Worse, you're not sure how to go about getting it.

Let's change that.

In these pages, I'll help you build a better mousetrap to make sure, as my company slogan puts it, you'll "be heard." You'll learn how strategically crafted and applied public relations can buttress your brand and amplify your message. Effective PR is neither rocket science nor dumb luck; it is the wise leveraging of expectations and opportunities. I'll say it again for emphasis and to ensure a clean page break: *Effective PR is neither rocket science nor dumb luck; it is the wise leveraging of expectations and opportunities.* It is simple, but not easy. It is best played as a team sport, not a solo one. You realize that already if you're reading this sentence all the way to this period. Congratulations. And thank you. I'm honored you've chosen me as your teammate. Well, maybe I'm more of a coach— more on that later. For the time being, though, let's "Play ball!"

> **Effective PR is neither rocket science nor dumb luck; it is the wise leveraging of expectations and opportunities.**

We'll start at the beginning—literally. As in "In the beginning," drawing from biblical history to see that Moses was the first person to find himself in your position of needing a little help to carry out his calling and disseminate his message. That's right. Cecil B. DeMille left that part out of *The Ten Commandments*, but we'll cover it here. We'll do so as part of our examination of just why PR is so important on your journey to— forgive me—the Promised Land. I'll explain why advertising will never do for you what public relations can. And I'll introduce you to something I call PR pottery-making: how to turn your desire into content on which you can paint a message that will attract attention to your unique work of art.

We'll also look at the environment into which you'll be placing your message. Hint: It's not what you think it is. And that's a good thing for reasons I'll explain. Then we'll talk about how you need to know with laser-like focus and precision, before you step into that environment, what you offer and stand for—whether you're an author, expert, speaker, coach, consultant or some mash-up of all of them. The marketplace of ideas is a crowded, noisy place, and chances are you'll need to do a little fine-tuning of what you're offering to make maximum sales.

The meat-and-potatoes portion of our program follows—an in-depth examination of how to craft a strategy that turns opportunity into achievements. I'll share real-life examples from my 15 years as a journalist and 15 more as a PR guy, a journey that took me from my hometown paper to Hollywood, from writing stories that got delivered to my doorstep to being interviewed for stories that got broadcast around the world. From being praised by Sean Hannity and Roma

Downey to being savaged by Keith Olbermann (who named me the Second Worst Person in the World) and Howard Stern (who called me a bunch of names I'll have to spell with &*%$#@!*& in case your kids pick up the book.) Some of those stories will spotlight how to do PR right, and some will wincingly reveal what happens when you do PR wrong. A few might even include the name "Donald Trump." Here's the good news: In addition to giving you something to chuckle about at my expense, they'll prove that very few mistakes in the communications business are fatal if you're honest and prepared.

We'll wrap up by touching on how to build on what you build, not just creating but maintaining momentum that ensures your message consistently cuts through the word noise, and does so with boldness and creative clarity. Good communication isn't a shouting match, but sometimes it pays to be loud—I did name my firm ROAR, after all. It's OK, even sometimes necessary, to blow the other guy's hair back a little bit with the power of your message.

One last parenthetical note. Sprinkled throughout you'll find what I call *PR-Verbs*, a.k.a., public-relations proverbs—scraps of wisdom I've picked up and passed along over the last three decades. I'm not talking about quotes from the text in bigger type like the one several sentences back; these will be additional content, flinty bits of insight along the lines of "A bird in the hand is worth two in the bush" or "You can lead a horse to water, but you can't make him drink"—but unpacked a bit more and geared toward bringing you to a deeper understanding of this profession I love so dearly.

All right, then, turn the page and let's get ... kidding! I know I still need to explain what the heck the book's title means, like I promised at the outset. You don't really think I'd forget that, do you? That would have undercut everything I've done so far to try to convince you of my credibility and authority to be advising you about communications. I'm just trying to be clever. Occupational hazard.

MEANWHILE, BACK AT THE DAWN OF MY CAREER AND THIS INTRO

I first heard about "biting the dog" in the late '80s, a kid just out of college in his first newspaper gig. It was explained to me, a cub reporter covering the police beat, that the things I needed to be looking for were "man-bites-dog" stories. That's an old journalism aphorism for the truth that a collection of facts and actions is not worth the ink to print it or the airwaves to broadcast it (today we'd say the pixels to publish it) if it's a "dog-bites-man" story. Why? Because dogs have been biting men since the two species first got a look at each other. It is an unsurprising outcome—even an expected one in some cases. It's a waste of the reporter's time to even look up from her notebook, the newsroom argument goes, when a canine sets its canines into a human. Yawn. Next.

But if a man bites a dog? Stop the presses. Cut into *The Big Bang Theory* with a breaking-news alert. Cue Matt Drudge to slap those flashing police lights on his website that signal Newsmageddon. When a man bites a dog, the unexpected has happened— and news cycles run on the unexpected. Sometimes, you find it in a situation, like the Chicago Cubs winning the 2016 World Series. That's a man-bites-dog story because the last time they did it was 108 years earlier, and in the decades afterward fans and media alike attributed the drought

The Chicago Cubs' 2016 World Series win was such a man-bites-dog story, the team plastered a full-size front-page of the *Chicago Tribune* documenting the feat inside Wrigley Field. The author, a huge Cubs fan, later prodded his wife into posing with him in front of it.
(Personal photo.)

to a curse that would never be broken. Broken curses—those are sure to get a dog chomped on.

Sometimes it's individual behavior that qualifies. Remember Susan Boyle? Back in 2009, she was a contestant on *Britain's Got Talent*, one of those reality competition shows where half the auditioning acts are purposely awful to give audiences something to laugh at and someone to feel superior to. Producers portrayed Boyle in the segment that introduced her as the epitome of awful—overweight, frumpy, a bit socially awkward. Simon Cowell, reality TV's hangin' judge, rolled his eyes when she took the stage. Then she sang. Like an angel.[3] Susan Boyle went on to build a career of enviable strength and length—in part on the purity of her voice, in part on the fact that such purity is unexpected from "someone like her." She's a man-bites-dog success story.

This doesn't mean you have to win the World Series long after anyone thought you could. It doesn't mean you have to sing like Sinatra or Streisand in their primes. It doesn't even mean, if I may step out from behind the Wizard's curtain for a moment, that every story you ever see, hear or read involves a human nibbling on a Shih Tzu. Truth is, some news just is— governments raise taxes, disasters strike, pop-culture trends occur, and journalists write about them because they figure their audiences will care. You may wind up featured in those kinds of stories by default, because your area of expertise aligns with the reporter's area of need. But stories of that stripe will not sustain your profile as an author, expert, speaker, coach or consultant. If you want it, you can't wait for it. You have to go get it. And the best way (the only way, really) to get it and hang on to it is to leverage the expectations of the news media—the people you want to cover your message —to spotlight the ways in which you exceed or defy those expectations. It requires dedicated thought and action to get there. After all, dog bites just happen. For man bites you need a plan.

I had one, and had been executing it for months, when Jim Daly rolled his Harley. Because I was both prepared and practiced in *the wise leveraging of expectations and opportunities* through *strategically crafted and applied public relations,* I was able to transform a dog-bites-man story into a man-bites-dog story. It could have been a run-of-the-mill brief about an accident involving the new CEO of the ministry whose radio show your parents listened to; it became a Page 1 pronouncement that this organization, now led by a young guy with oodles of moxie, isn't the same stale outfit your parents flocked to. That framing—we'll talk about this word many more times as an alternative to "spin" and its myriad negative connotations—will help you make news with your message. And making news with your message will help you make something that matters with it.

And that's why we're all here, isn't it?

1

Of Biblical Proportions

I've got good news for you. If you're at your wit's end about how to influence an audience with the message that reflects your heart's desire, I'm going help you fight the good fight. We won't get you there just by the skin of your teeth, either, because this is not the blind leading the blind. PR is a labor of love for me. I promise to go the extra mile in these pages to make sure your house is in order when it comes to reaching and influencing the powers that be.

Sound good? It should. I stole most of it from the best-selling book in history.

Let's revisit that paragraph with the words and phrases I swiped highlighted: I've got *good news* for you. If you're *at your wit's end* about how to influence an audience with the message that reflects your *heart's desire*, I'm going help you *fight the good fight*. We won't get you there just *by the skin of your teeth*, either, because this is not *the blind leading the blind*. PR is a *labor of love* for me. I promise to *go the extra mile* in these pages to make sure *your house is in order* when it comes to reaching and influencing *the powers that be*.

And that's just a drop in the bucket when it comes to everyday words and phrases that originated in, you guessed it, the Bible. (In fact, *a drop in the bucket* is another one. OK, I'll stop now.)

This point was one I helped Roma Downey and her husband, Mark Burnett, make in a man-bites-dog opinion piece for *The Wall Street Journal*. The couple, she the actress of *Touched by an Angel* fame and he the creative force behind such reality TV hits as *Survivor, Shark Tank* and *The Voice*, were looking to make a splash with their HISTORY Channel miniseries, *The Bible*. To do so, they needed a hook to knock the press's and the public's expectations askew. That's when we hit upon the idea of a piece that argued the Bible should be taught in US schools, possibly even made mandatory. It was a bold argument in a society that places such importance on the popular understanding of the separation of church and state, but it worked because the whole point of the essay was that the Bible has immense value that extends beyond its spiritual content.

"We're not talking about religion here, and certainly not about politics. We're talking about knowledge," Downey and Burnett wrote. "The foundations of knowledge of the ancient world—which informs the understanding of the modern world—are biblical in origin. Teddy Roosevelt, the 26th president known more as a cigar-chomping Rough Rider than a hymn-singing Bible-thumper, once said: 'A thorough knowledge of the Bible is worth more than a college education.'

"Can you imagine students not reading the Constitution in a US government class?" they added. "School administrators not sharing the periodic table of the elements with their science classes? A driver's ed course that expected young men and women to pass written and road tests without having access to a booklet enumerating the rules of the road?"[4]

How about someone hoping to understand and leverage the power of PR, but not studying the first person of impact and influence to need and secure public-relations assistance?

Don't worry about that last one. We're going to talk about it right now.

SLOW OF TONGUE, QUICK TO SEEK HELP

You may know Moses from Sunday school, or from Michelangelo's brilliant painting on the ceiling of the Sistine Chapel (one of the most familiar masterpieces of the art world), or as Charlton Heston with a skunk stripe in his hair and supposedly stone tablets in his arms in *The Ten Commandments*. He is a figure of titanic importance in Judaism and Christianity, a man chosen by God to lead an oppressed people out of slavery into freedom. In the Bible, he is the Old Testament figure most mentioned in the New Testament; in the Quran, his name turns up more than anybody else's—including Muhammad's.

Among the many titles Moses has been given by posterity—Deliverer, Prophet, Lawgiver—we must add one: First PR Client.

We're not going over any of this for religious purposes. We're interested in the historical weight of the man. He was, after all, depicted on the first seal of the United States by Founding Fathers John Adams, Thomas Jefferson and Benjamin Franklin— the guys who wrote the Declaration of Independence![5] And among the many titles Moses has been given by posterity—Deliverer, Prophet, Lawgiver—we must add one: First PR Client.

That's because Moses, for all the leadership qualities that got him chosen by God to lead the Israelites to the Promised Land, knew there was one thing he could not do by himself: He didn't trust his ability to speak to the people he was called to lead in a way that would marshal them to action. By the biblical account, Moses is commissioned by the Almighty in Exodus Chapter 4. He immediately begins to muse aloud about whether he's up for the task, prompting God to show him a couple of miracles sure to get the people's attention: turning his shepherd's staff into a snake then back again and giving him leprosy of the hand that He cures by having Moses slip it under his cloak. God even promises a third miracle if the first two don't cut it with the masses: If Moses pours water from the Nile on the ground before them, it will turn into blood.

But Moses still waffles. All the signs and wonders in the world, he sheepishly tells God, will not help him overcome his ineloquence, a condition he describes in Verse 10 as "being slow of speech and tongue." He goes so far as to try to beg off the assignment altogether. He asks God to select someone else for what was, at the time, at least equal to Noah's building and piloting of the ark as *literally* the most important job in history. That's how certain Moses was that his communication skills weren't up to snuff, and that communication skills were going to be a major part of the uprooting and transplantation of more than a million men, women and children out of Egypt and into Canaan.

It's at this precise moment the Creator of the Universe became the Creator of Public Relations.

"What about your brother, Aaron? I know he can speak well," God says in Chapter 4, Verse 14. "You shall speak to him and put words in his mouth."

We're already running the risk of this becoming a theology lesson, so we'll speed up the narrative here. Aaron starts by going with his brother to the Israelites and sharing God's plan for their deliverance. The arrangement works well: The people catch the vision for leaving under Moses' leadership; Aaron helps Moses make increasingly compelling cases to Pharaoh about why he should "let their people go" (side note: it's not the PR person's fault if the audience doesn't grasp the importance of the message, which in this case was, "You will suffer under plagues of, among other things, hail, locusts, darkness, frogs, boils and the death of everybody's first-born child"); and the Exodus gets under way, including the perilous parting of and passage through the Red Sea.

Two instances of Aaron's value as Moses' PR representative are worth singling out. In the first, the Israelites are getting testy because they're hungry—actually complaining about how good their stomachs had it as slaves. So Moses tells Aaron to let them know God has heard their grumbling. The Lord's response? He will present them with nutritional provisions nightly in the form of quail that fly in and a honey wafer called manna that will be deposited literally from heaven. In the second instance, the wanderers are attacked by the desert tribesmen whose land they're passing through; Moses leads the fight by standing on a rock and raising his hands above his head as a sign of reliance on God. As long as his hands are aloft, the Israelites are winning. But when his arms get tired and drop to his side as the skirmish drags on, Aaron and another of Moses' lieutenants have to prop them up to ensure victory.

Alas, Aaron is not destined to keep his PR job throughout the journey—which may or may not be why it takes the group 40 years to get where it's going. Moses basically reassigns his big brother to another role—as one of the community's priests. Why? Maybe he was

Moses and Aaron Speak to the People, c. 1896-1902, by James Jacques Joseph Tissot (French, 1836-1902), gouache on board, 8 7/16 x 10 1/8 in. (21.4 x 25.7 cm), at the Jewish Museum, New York.

emboldened by the initial successes of the arrangement, perhaps thinking he'd learned enough to go it alone delivering God's messages to the people. What isn't in doubt is the disastrous outcome of the decision. Episode after episode follows in which Moses, who first exhibits his hair-trigger temper when he kills a slave master all the way back in Exodus 2, gets in arguments with the people. Aaron, perhaps distraught at losing his communications responsibilities, engages in a little blasphemous behavior of his own. The entire ebb and flow of the brothers' story ends where it began: standing in front of the people Moses has been called to lead, needing to communicate and carry out an important message from God. It goes as badly as it possibly could.

All Moses needs to do, per God's instruction, is call water out from a rock to quench the thirst of the yet-again bellyaching Israelites.

Aaron is standing beside his brother, but says nothing and does less, as Moses ignores God's instructions. He doesn't call water from the rock but smacks it instead with his staff. That does, indeed, produce the promised water—but also brings grave consequences for our fraternal heroes. They will be allowed to complete the duty of leading the people to the Promised Land, but they are personally forbidden from entering. Moses and Aaron die without ever having stepped sandal in Canaan, never able to enjoy the fruits of their labor.

See how high the stakes can be in the PR game? You might even say wisely leveraging expectations and opportunities—my definition of effective PR from the introduction—is a matter of biblical importance.

IF NO ONE HEARS/SEES/READS IT, DO YOU ACTUALLY SAY/WRITE IT?

Two of the key takeaways from the tale of Moses and Aaron are that having something to say isn't enough to ensure your message is heard and acted on—not even if God Himself put that message in your heart; and, if you want to reach "enough," you need help—someone to hold up your arms when you get weary to ensure victory in the battle.

So, would it be fair to conclude that having something to say is just half the battle of effective PR?

No.

That's because strategically crafted and applied public relations isn't a function of two halves, but three thirds.

Having something to say is a third of the battle. Having something people want and need to hear is another third. Saying it in a way that arrests their

> **Having something to say is a third of the battle. Having something people want and need to hear is another third. Saying it in a way that arrests their imaginations and understanding is the final third.**

imaginations and understanding is the final third. The first speaks to your *desire*; the second to your *content*; the third to your *message*. Each builds upon the other to get you to that place we've identified where your message consistently cuts through the word noise, and does so with boldness and creative clarity. Let's unpack each step of the process to give you a better roadmap for your own journey to a land flowing with milk and honey.

1. *Having something to say is a third of the battle.* You wouldn't be reading this book if you weren't here already. Congrats. That means you're 33 percent of the way through your journey. If this were Monopoly, you'd be sauntering past States Avenue on your way to Virginia Avenue, the magical jackpot space of Free Parking within eyeshot up ahead.

    You want to help people. You want to make a name for yourself. You wouldn't mind earning a little money while you do it. There are opinions and observations and insights and expertise bubbling up inside you, and you may burst if you don't get them all out.

    I've worked with plenty of thought leaders like you. Ideas drop into your head like that manna we talked about dropping from heaven for Moses and Aaron and the Israelites. Sometimes it feels like too much —and it might be. Keeping what you want to say focused can be tough sometimes. One of my clients and I refer to this three-step process of making news that matters as PR pottery-making.

    Here at Step 1 we're putting together the clay. This is the ball of ideas from which we're going to sculpt our content, then paint it with our message. We hunker down for strategy sessions where we look to narrow the scope of all his passion. He'll be tossing out ideas and realize he's adding more clay to the raw material, not shaving any away. That's all right, I assure him. It just ensures we have enough to make the most detailed sculpture possible. He laughs ... and tosses in a couple more wads of clay.

This is how the first third ought to be. We should always aim for building the biggest ball of clay we can. You never want to rush a piece of art—be it a sculpture or the content you want to unleash on the marketplace of ideas.

2. *Having something to say that people want and need to hear is another third.*

    Here's where the work and the fun get going in earnest. We start whittling away at that ball of clay, shaping what you want to say into something that in form and function people want and need to hear. In a Monopoly game, these are the few dice rolls to get you to Ventnor Avenue and the lobby of the Water Works—tonier neighborhoods, pricier properties. All the signs of just about having "arrived."

    What it looks like in PR practice is very much what it looks like in PR pottery-making. Finer and finer details emerge about the work you want to put out there for all see. Tough decisions get made here—decisions about what your identity and goals need to be to reach the biggest audience and the most customers; about what differentiates you from the competition and why those differences will make the masses part with their time, attention and money. We've talked a few times about leveraging expectations and opportunities. This is where we build the muscle to achieve that leverage.

    A word of warning or encouragement, depending on how you take it: Something you want to say will be eliminated from consideration at this stage. Pieces of clay you really like, chunks even, will wind up on the art studio floor. But take heart: Discarding them leaves you with a kiln-ready creation the people you want to reach will love.

BE LIKE NIKE: JUST DO IT

You can't do PR without doing interviews. I've done hundreds in my career, and, yes, sometimes they can be intimidating. So here's a never-fails tip for making sure that you, not the journalist asking the questions, are in charge when you chat. Are you ready? You might even want to get a highlighter out.

Do the interview.

Yep, that's it. By just doing the interview, you ensure you are in control. It is a fallacy that the journalist "runs the show." Lord knows there are battalions of aggressive ones out there who like to cajole and push and "ask the tough questions"—but the reality is you're in charge, not them. Always. Every time.

Here's why. They need you to do their job. Without the things you have to say to populate their story, they have no story. They have the ability to ask the questions, yes, but that's where their influence on you ends. You, though, have the ability to a) answer those questions or not; and most importantly b) decide how to answer them. All the power lies on your side of the ledger.

3. *Saying it in a way that arrests their imaginations and understanding is the final third.*

We start the final third of our journey with a finished sculpture. You now know exactly what it is you'll be putting on display. This is the highest-octane part of the Monopoly board—Boardwalk and Park Place, but also Jail and Luxury Tax. Big rewards. Big potential pitfalls. A lot riding on each roll of the dice. But always shining ahead of you: Go. The ultimate goal of each rotation. With a little reward every time you achieve it. The high satisfaction of high stakes.

It's time for the artist in you to step forward in PR pottery-making. You've got a finished whole, but what parts do you want those who look at it to always remember? Put a little bit more shading here, a little bit more color there. Add details that reinforce its uniqueness and appeal. Flicks of the brush only you can apply. It's your final chance to make a lasting impression with your work. Don't miss an opportunity to stand out.

No step is more critical than this one in your effort to, as the subtitle of this book puts it, unleash the power of PR to make news that matters. Doing so will require you to be all in, because PR is not a one-off. Each day brings new opportunities and challenges. Each day requires new energy and effort. Each day offers up another dog to bite.

PR WILL GET YOU TO THE PROMISED LAND TODAY

By now you may be asking yourself, "Can't I just pay to get the exposure I need for my (fill in the blank)? Why go through all this work trying to get a TV show or radio program or online publication or newspaper or magazine to cover my (fill in the blank), when I can reach plenty of ears and eyeballs through advertising? I mean, it seems to work pretty well for all those companies that shell out $5 million for 30–second spots during the Super Bowl every year."

You're right, of course. Advertising is always an option—and not a fruitless one. As a thought leader looking to hang out a shingle in the marketplace of ideas, chances are you can generate some traction with well-constructed and -targeted spots. But you should know there's a bigger difference between *paid media* (advertising) and *earned media* (coverage) than whether you have to write a check to get into or onto an outlet's platform.

You've certainly figured out that the recommendation of this book will not be for you to go it alone as an untrained practitioner of PR. So you surely understand this: The odds are good, unless you have family in the business or some sort of barter system with friends through which you swap services, that you're going to have to spend some money to secure experienced and capable PR help. It will almost surely cost you a mere fraction of what advertising does, but that's not even the point. You can, using industry-standard software and formulas, even arrive at a number that allows you to assign monetary value to the coverage you earn, but even that isn't the point. The point is it will be exponentially more valuable to you.

But don't take my word for it.

A 2014 study by Nielsen on the role of content in the consumer decision-making process concluded that PR is almost 90 percent more effective than advertising.[6] "On average, expert content lifted familiarity 88 percent more than branded content," the report concluded. Robert Wynne, a contributor to *Forbes* magazine, which published the study's findings, added that he thought Nielsen's number was low.

"With advertising, you tell people how great you are," he said. "With publicity, others sing your praises. Which do you think is more effective?"[7]

Before you answer, check out what Crosby Noricks, writing for the Independent Fashion Bloggers, says:

> Implied third-party endorsement by an editor can carry more credibility among potential customers. For example, let's imagine a young, professional woman flipping through *Lucky Magazine*. A full-page advertisement from Diane von Furstenberg featuring a wine-colored wrap dress may have less impact on her than if a fashion editor lists the dress as her 'fall must-have,' noting the flattering shape. The idea here is that the editor is a fashionable, industry expert, and as such that editor wields a greater influence on our young professional friend, flipping through the magazine for a dress she is looking to wear to her job interview next week.[8]

Here's a simple way of encapsulating the difference: *Advertising builds awareness; PR builds affinity.* Both are megaphones that can

> Advertising builds awareness; PR builds affinity. Both are megaphones that can amplify your message, but only one makes you sound sweeter.

amplify your message, and there are compelling arguments to be made that pairing them up helps your voice carry farther, but only one makes you sound sweeter to the folks who are listening. If you want someone to know about your brand or service, the best avenue is the ad department. If you want someone to like your brand or service a little bit more than he likes your competition's, give the newsroom a shout. (Later on, I will unpack a mammoth case study of this truth from Super Bowl XLIV, when I worked for Focus on the Family. We bought an ad during the game featuring Heisman Trophy winner Tim Tebow — at a price tag of about $3 million, no pittance for a nonprofit organization. But we drummed up more than 10 times that in earned media coverage — about $35 million when we stopped counting — by leveraging some pretty entrenched expectations about who we were as a Christian ministry. We bit the dog — hard and often — and it resulted in some truly remarkable exposure for our programs and services. And led to that Howard Stern tirade I mentioned. You can watch it here: www.bit.ly/BTDstern. Just wear headphones or turn down the sound. And keep the little ones away.)

This truth that both paid and earned media give you a stage, but coverage invariably leads to more applause than advertising, applies even/especially in the world of new/social media. We'll get into this in greater detail in chapter 2, when we examine the media landscape that exists today and the myriad opportunities for you to plug into it. For now, know that what was true in 1818 when the *New-York Columbian* did a story on Dr. James Blundell performing the first blood transfusion will be true in 2018 if *This American Life* features you on its weekly podcast. Two hundred years of history and all the technological advances they've wrought have not put a dent in it being more impressive to audiences when someone else spotlights you than when you spotlight yourself.

Just remember: Your job is to be in that spotlight. Somebody else should be operating it, a trained technician and tactician, somebody who will make sure the light is shining on your best side with the satisfactory number of lumens. We're mixing our generations here, but don't forget you're Moses. You need an Aaron.

NEXT UP

If biting a dog were easy, well, then there'd be no man-bites-dog stories, and I would have had to pick one of my backup titles, like *Message in a Bottle Rocket*, for this book. Truth is, it's hard. Not just literally. That's why the figurative practice is called *earned* media. You have to earn it. And if earning it were a cinch, marketing textbooks would be calling it "found media" or "dropped-in-your-lap media." It requires hard work to wisely leverage expectations and opportunities (that phrase, I hope, is going to be an earworm to you, like an early Madonna song, by the time we're done.)

Our first task: studying just what the expectations and opportunities are in the modern mediasphere. Hold your preconceptions loosely—you're going to lose some of them as we go.

2

(Not) As Seen on TV

I love superheroes (You probably figured that out when you saw the cover of this book). Superman is my favorite. He has been since the 1978 movie starring Christopher Reeve. Its posters promised "You'll believe a man can fly!"—and this 13-year-old moviegoer palpitatingly did. Even today, after 40 years of technological advances in special effects, with CGI images decades ago replacing actors in even the most pedestrian motion-picture action sequences, my heart still skips a beat when the Man of Steel floats onto the balcony of Lois Lane's penthouse apartment for his first big interview with the *Daily Planet*.

While my love of the Last Son of Krypton and my affection for the film have not abated through three sequels and two big-screen reboots, one aspect of *Superman: The Movie* does trouble the 30-years-in-journalism-and-PR moviegoer in me: the terrible reporting skills of Lois, and Clark Kent (Superman's alter ego—shhh, don't tell anybody.) I can forgive the running gag that Lois can't spell and the one-off joke that Clark's most impressive qualification for his job, considering he has no chasing-the-story experience, is that he's the fastest typist Perry White has ever seen. All that aside, neither demonstrates the slightest reportorial instinct or savvy—and I'm not just talking about Lois being clueless that her colleague with the big glasses and bumbling demeanor is actually the dreamy hero she's in love with.

The interview she conducts with Superman after he flies onto her penthouse landing tells the tale. She asks him how tall he is and how

> **The media environment you're aiming to plant your message into is not as you've been led to believe by popular media portrayals.**

much he weighs, whether he's married, how old he is (he suavely declines to answer), even if he … eats. She coyly asks about his relationship status (he coyly responds he's single but she'll be the first to know if that changes.) She does eventually get around to asking him where he's from (he explains he's a visitor from another planet, Krypton, which she originally spells Cripton) and why he's come to earth (to fight for truth, justice and the American way, which she mocks as naïve.) But watch the scene for yourself (Google "superman lois lane balcony scene") and you'll see she asks no follow-up questions, shows not a whit of interest in his motives for going after bad guys or why he chose to save humanity in Metropolis as opposed to, say, Gotham City. There's not a single thing she gets her subject to say that she could actually use as a direct quote in a news story. She's the journalism equivalent to Lex Luthor's bumbling sidekick, Otis.

Confession: I'm not being totally serious in this analysis. I get that the point of the interview isn't investigative reportage, but a meet-cute between our hero and his gal. Still, there is a legitimate undercurrent to our discussion: The media environment you're aiming to plant your message into is not as you've been led to believe by popular media portrayals. Movies, TV, books, even news outlets themselves and the pundits who populate them, mischaracterize the sandbox you'll be playing in.

JUST SAY 'NOPE' TO OLIVIA POPE

It's not quite as easy to find entertainment depictions of PR professionals. The "Hollywood press agent" was a fairly common supporting character in '40s and '50s films about the industry itself—whether he was helping Don Lockwood keep arsenic-voiced Lina LaMont from crooning onscreen in *Singin' in the Rain* or mourning the death of the starlet he loved while investigating small-town miracles with a quiet priest played by Frank Sinatra (!) in *Miracle of the Bells*. It's been far more common, on the big and small screens, to see characters whose work dabs around the edges of public relations but goes by another name: crisis manager or image consultant or fixer or political strategist. In nearly every instance, the characters are amoral or immoral, conniving and corrupt, not only willing but eager to play fast and loose with the facts and the law to get their clients out of trouble, into office or over on the masses whose money they crave.

This is typified nowhere better than in ABC's hit drama *Scandal*, whose central character, Olivia Pope, fulfills all the roles mentioned two sentences above. Full disclosure: I don't watch *Scandal*. But I know her firm of "gladiators in suits"[9] has, over its seven-season run, erased evidence, leaked made-up stories that not only killed opponents' careers but got them incarcerated, and hidden bodies slain by their clients. Olivia herself? She's slept with those who've hired her (including the president of the United States), leveraging the clandestine relationships to advance her own lust for power. Oh, yeah, she's also beaten a man to death with a chair. We're not talking a figurative biting of a dog here. We're talking napalming a litter of puppies.

Let's agree to toss these distorted examples of the press and PR landscapes onto the ash heap—I just realized Showtime's hit *Ray Donovan* fits the bill, too—or at least leave them in the DVR. We're looking to make some moves, and some waves, and some news, in the real world, not the reel world. The opportunities are endless there, and the people are pretty professional and personable. Onward!

GET YOUR FILL AT THE NEWS BUFFET

If you've never eaten at a Las Vegas casino buffet, and you're not concerned about a five-figure caloric intake just this once, then I'm tempted to say put the book down and get thee to Caesars Palace.

There really is nothing like the layout, and outlay, of consumables at the biggest players on the Strip. Consider:

> Caesars Palace's Bacchanal Buffet is a mammoth 25,000-square-foot room with nine different show kitchens, including Mexican, Italian, Chinese, Japanese, American, seafood, pizza, deli (including soups, cheeses and charcuterie selections) and desserts. All the 'comfort foods'—from mac 'n' cheese and mashed potatoes to prime rib—are served. Each show kitchen also has an action station with plated dishes and 'minis' (small-sized portions of modern cuisine to tempt foodies—like red velvet pancakes, oak-grilled lamb chops and roasted South Carolina shrimp and grits.) Among the uniquely crafted items, guests will discover house-smoked barbecue ribs and brisket, fresh tortillas and oyster shucking.[10]

Hungry yet?

You should be, and not just for "charcuterie selections," whatever the heck they are. Your mouth should be watering at the prospect of filling your PR plate with the breadth and variety waiting for you at the modern-day news buffet. There, you'll find as many distinct media outlet channel types as the Caesars Bacchanal has kitchens: local and national television; local, regional and national radio; local and national newspapers and magazines; blogs; podcasts; and an essentially bottomless tray of social media platforms. Some of these are run by wealthy individuals and corporations with stockholders and thousands of employees; some are run by your friends and neighbors, with day jobs and

Some of the most influential news sources today aren't run out of New York or Los Angeles; they're run out of somebody's studio apartment.

two or three kids. This is not your parents' (or your grandparents') mediasphere—when it wasn't news if Walter Cronkite didn't say that's the way it was. Some of the most influential news sources today aren't run out of New York or Los Angeles; they're run out of somebody's studio apartment. And all of them are viable avenues for you to get your message out.

The expansion and diversification of news media hasn't just resulted in a bigger and better buffet. It's also seen the rise of unique artisan offerings— media channels of all outlet types that specialize in niche content. Cable business networks, faith-centric websites, ideologically conservative and liberal blogs, streaming radio stations and not just sports podcasts, but baseball, football, basketball, hockey and even jai alai podcasts.

Let's camp out here for a moment, to spotlight the ever-widening opportunities out there for you in this new normal. According to a 2016 Pew study, about one in five US adults 12 or older (21 percent) listened to some kind of podcast in the past month, up from 12 percent six years ago; 36 percent have listened to a podcast ever, up from 23 percent in 2010.[11] Here's the even better news: Pew also found that even though the audience (and revenue) for podcasts is only a slice of that for radio, streaming radio has been growing as well. The share who listened to online radio (whether news or non-news) in the past month more than doubled since 2010, from 27 percent to 57 percent. This growth hasn't cannibalized the audience for traditional radio, though. Ninety-one percent of those 12 and older listened to terrestrial radio in the past month. When it comes to news radio in particular, NPR's flagship news programs each have about 12 million listeners. (That's roughly half of the average viewership of the three nightly TV network newscasts, which together attracted about 24 million viewers in 2015.)[12]

Did you get all that? The rocketing growth of podcasts isn't stealing from the audiences for new (streaming) or traditional (over-the-air) radio. It actually seems to be creating a greater thirst for news, which creates fresh opportunities for you as someone who wants to make news. I'm not exaggerating when I say that whatever your area of expertise as an author, expert, speaker, coach and/or consultant, there exists, in this smorgasbord of newsmaking options, any number of national and major marketplaces to tell your story, as well as an equal or even greater number of audience- and interest-specific niche options. Let's break down that latter category a bit, because there are important differences in the two main types of outlets you'll discover there.

PITCH YOUR NICHE

Old-school industry and hobby media. Here you'll find the generations-old media that pinpoint a clientele based on what they do for a living or for fun. This is the home to outlets focused on boating, insurance, cigars, biking, food, and on and on. To secure coverage here, a major aspect of the news you're making must hit the bullseye of the industry or hobby being celebrated. Your expertise as a fitness instructor or home-organization guru, no matter how artfully you bite the dog, is not going to make it into *Classic Trucks Magazine* or the *Grammar Girl Quick and Dirty Tips for Better Writing* podcast.

But you can find success if you're in the topic ZIP code of the outlet: Fitness instructors can land exposure in *Cruise Travel Magazine* if they can convince editors to do a story on maintaining an exercise routine at sea. Home organizers have a shot at *Field & Stream* if they come up with a better system for storing gear during a hunting off-season.

General news "directed reporting." These niche outlets, newer to the scene than those described above, cover general-interest news and events. But they do so unapologetically through an ideological or religious lens. No, I'm not talking about the Fox News Channel or CNN—liberals bash the former and conservatives the latter for being politically biased in their reporting. That is overwhelmingly not the case; these media make every attempt to tell, and succeed most of the time in telling, news stories that cover all sides of an issue.

Not so "directed reporting," which exists to advance a viewpoint without feeling the need to offer the "other side" equal time to balance or counter it. You'll see it most often in most forms of religious media and political and cultural websites not affiliated with corporate news organizations. They have an agenda and are not shy about acknowledging it. They do true reporting—interviewing sources, covering breaking news, presenting features that spotlight people doing interesting things. But every piece has a thread running through it that makes clear they believe their way of looking at the world is what's best for the world. Atheists are unlikely to get positive coverage for their cause from the Christian Broadcasting Network; liberals are unlikely to get it from *TownHall.com*.

You're going to need to sup in the dining rooms of both mass market and niche media if you hope to be as successful as you want to be in your—here comes that phrase again—wise leveraging of expectations and opportunities as you seek to make news that matters. It's like walking—you go farther and faster on two legs. If you're just hopping around on one foot, you have a tendency to go in circles, and you're probably going to fall down a time or two.

We can return to Superman, believe it or not, to illustrate this point. In 2013, when Warner Bros. was marketing *Man of Steel*, its latest reboot of the character, the studio focused its advertising dollars and in-house PR/publicity teams on generating awareness and affinity in the massive dining halls where *The Tonight Show, Ellen* and *The New York Times* hang out. But it also hired on as promotional partners firms like the one I worked for at the time, Grace Hill Media, which specializes in getting both paid and earned media from the artisan kitchens of faith-based media outlets. *Man of Steel* was an ideal project for us—Superman is, after all, the story of an otherworldly father who sends his only son to Earth to save mankind, a concept quite familiar to followers of Jesus Christ. We helped Warner Bros. build positive buzz in the Christian niche market in the same way the studio's own efforts focused on general market awareness and affinity. The results of the dual strategy speak for themselves: $291 million in domestic box office receipts, good for the fifth highest-grossing movie of the year.

Oh, and the project netted my firm a nice little nip at the dog. The idea that Christendom in general and churches specifically were teaming up with Hollywood, long criticized by people of faith for the risqué content of its product, ran contrary to the media's preconceptions about how the two sides would get along if left alone in the same room, let alone working on the same movie. So we leveraged the expectation of hostility and got the story of the partnership not just told, but told in the pages of *USA Today*, with its 2.3 million readers.

"Take it as a sign of the changing times that a secular movie is being embraced as a teaching opportunity for Christians, not ignored or condemned as it might have been in the past as a threat to godly values from an evil Hollywood," columnist Tom Krattenmaker wrote. "Credit the change instigators in evangelical America for a new understanding that it's better to engage the wider culture than hunker behind a wall of insularity. After all, you can't learn from, or influence, that which you shun."[13]

RULES OF ENGAGEMENT

Content is king for every one of these outlets—from *The Wall Street Journal* to *The Homeschool Mommy Blog*. You must always remember you are no longer just an author, expert, speaker, coach or consultant. You are no longer solely a content provider through the distribution channels you control—your website, blog, podcast, social media pages or books. You are now—don't laugh—a media personality. You've heard the phrase, in reference to actors and actresses, that they are *bankable* stars? You are now a *bookable* spokesperson. In a very real sense, the media outlets you are looking to land in to spread your message need you more than you need them—because there is no news without newsmakers. TV and radio shows have hours of programming to fill—day in, day out. Claim minutes of that time as your own. Publications, printed and digital, need millions of words to fill their pages and screens every day—most of them day in, day out. Claim a few hundred or a few thousand of those words as your own—and aim for day in, day out.

The Atlantic conducted an interesting analysis in 2016 about just how many helpings are dished out daily at some of the news buffet's biggest kitchens.[14] It found that *The Washington Post* staff creates 500 stories and videos each day. That's more than twice as many as its big-newspaper rivals *The New York Times* and *The Wall Street Journal*, which come in at 230 and 240, respectively. *The Times*, perhaps in keeping with its storied all-the-news-that's-fit-to-print motto, offered plenty of detail to its numbers, saying they represent "roughly 150 articles a day (Monday–Saturday), 250 articles on Sunday and 65 blog posts per day." Those numbers increased over half a decade, too. In 2010, the paper published about 170 pieces per day: about 150 on weekdays and about 300 on Sunday. The other outlet surveyed, the popular website *Buzzfeed*, offered the most meager pickings, just 220 daily. Of course I'm kidding when I say "meager." That's better than nine pieces of news per hour, an almost mind-boggling number until you consider *The Post* cooks up its news burgers and brioche at a rate of just about one per minute. Every minute. Every day. Nothing at Caesars Palace's Bacchanal Buffett makes it from stovetop to plate that fast. So who's truly more impressive?

Understanding what the news buffet is cooking is important, but you have to understand who the chefs are, too. The men and women who make up the press, according to CareerCast figures for 2017, hold the sixth (newspaper) and ninth (broadcast) most stressful jobs in America (but don't feel too bad for them—PR executives come in at No. 8.)[15] There were 32,900 working journalists domestically in 2016.[16] Demographically, they profile at a median age of 47, a little more than 6 in 10 are male, 92 percent are college graduates, and the median salary is more than $53,600 for men, $44,342 for women. And—a definite dog-bites-man story—about 80 percent of those who acknowledge a political affiliation are Democrats.[17]

IF A STORY IS EXACTLY LIKE YOU WANTED, IT'S NOT EXACTLY WHAT YOU WANTED

No matter how often you find yourself in the middle—or comprising the whole—of a news story, you'll likely experience equal parts exhilaration and trepidation over how it's going to turn out. Whether it's a live radio segment, a taped TV interview or some quotes you give to a magazine reporter, you're excited to get your message across but worried you won't. *Did I cover what I wanted to cover? Will viewers forgive that brain freeze as I was answering the first question? Will the reporter quote me accurately?*

Learn this now and save yourself some heartache later: You'll be disappointed by the result sometimes, and you'll be thrilled by it sometimes. If you're anything like me, you'll realize every now and then that you blew it (much more on that in Chapter 7.) An occasion may even come when you read, watch or listen and think, "Wow, that turned out exactly how I wanted it to! That story couldn't have been more perfect if I'd done it myself!"

Beware those moments. Here's why.

Perfection is an illusion. In PR, it can make you overconfident about your abilities and not cautious enough about the reporter doing your next interview. You can start to think you don't need to prepare, that you've "arrived," that you can do this in your sleep. Even more dangerous, you can think the reporter's job is to make you look good. It is not. A reporter's job is to get the story. The good ones, the ones you want writing about you, will ask tough questions to get it. You need to be ready to answer them.

And you know what? You should want to answer them. That's primarily why any story that turns out exactly like you wanted isn't exactly what you want. You should want to answer tough questions, because they keep you sharp and demonstrate you know your stuff. Reporters who don't challenge you, don't bring a little skepticism to their side of the questions, don't push you to articulate your positions with precision and conviction, make you lazy.

Laziness and a hot mic don't mix.

Portrait of the Author as a Young Man: Proof that I was not formally trained as a reporter is on vivid display here, as I break the cardinal rule of accident and incident coverage: stay out of the photographer's line of sight. I was thoroughly taught that lesson by the veteran shooter behind the lens of this photo, whose excellent picture my notebook and I ruined. It is stamped for all time with the date of my shame: Sept. 19, 1987.
(Personal photo.)

I say that's a dog-bites-man story because it's not surprising—not because it is irrefutable truth of the oft-mentioned demon of "media bias." No one who has hung around journalists for any period of time (and I've done it for more than 30 years, 15 as one of them, 15 as a PR guy) will bat an eye at a survey that finds only about one in five are Republicans. But it is an illogical and incorrect leap to assume—worse yet, to proclaim—a reporter's or editor's political affiliation renders them incapable of doing journalism that doesn't reflexively marginalize those of the other political affiliation. That's because—uncap your highlighter and start shading in right after this word—all journalists are biased, and that's what makes most of them fair.

A personal story to illustrate the point: My first newspaper job in the late '80s was as the backup cops-and-courts reporter for *The Journal Times*, a daily newspaper in Racine, Wisconsin. The first trial I ever covered (and I do mean the first; I graduated college with English and Education degrees and had planned to be a high school teacher) was of a man accused of sexually assaulting an elderly woman. As I sat in the second row of the courtroom, all of 22 inexperienced years old, listening to the alleged victim describe in detail the things the accused forced her to do, I was not the slightest bit objective. The lady testifying reminded me of my grandma, and I was seething in my emotional condemnation of the defendant. In my mind, he could not have been guiltier. I confessed that to my mentor, the main cops-and-courts reporter, who taught me the principle that guided the rest of my journalism career: Objectivity is impossible, but fairness is mandatory.

What that meant, as I sat in front of the keyboard to tap out my trial story, was that I made sure I included as much of the defense's argument and witnesses as I did of the prosecution's. It wasn't just about "equal time" — although, as I recall, I did make sure the number of words I gave to each side was almost identical. It also meant "equal quality" — meaning I used the best quotes I had from each side. No pitting the prosecution's most compelling comments against the defense's weakest rebuttals and thus tipping the scales in the direction my emotions told me was the right one. Leading the reader to a conclusion about what happened was not my job as a news reporter; my job was to be the readers' eyes and ears, to describe what happened in that courtroom devoid of the lens of my bias. Knowing that bias was there made me more determined to strip away the lens.

Several other newspapers followed after the *Quad-City Times*. *The Victoria Advocate*. The *Star-Herald*. The *Times Record News*. At each stop, as I advanced from the front lines of reporting to the desk job of editing, I remembered and applied the rule that I may never be objective, but I always had to be fair. And an Ivory Soap percentage—99 and 44/100 percent pure—of my colleagues applied that rule as well. Never once did we hold a secret meeting of the He Man

All journalists are biased, and that's what makes most of them fair. Objectivity is impossible, but fairness is mandatory.

Conservatives (or Liberals) Haters Club. Never once did we drop the needle or press play on Don Henley's scathing ditty "Dirty Laundry," twirling our Snidely Whiplash mustaches as we maniacally sang about how we were going to stick it to the people and organizations we covered. We had our opinions, strong ones to boot, and we didn't keep them to ourselves when we socialized. But on the clock, on deadline, we played it down the middle, because that's what those who taught us how to do the job had done.

I still think it's how it's done by those who do the job today. That's why I say that the journalists with whom you will engage as you strive to make news that matters will almost all fall somewhere along the continuum of Best Friends Forever and Spawns of Satan. Which means your behavior should fall somewhere along the continuum of trusting them implicitly and being convinced they are out to ruin you and everything you believe in and stand for. The wise leveraging of expectations and opportunities — is there an echo in here? — doesn't just happen within those margins; it flourishes.

EXTREMELY IMPORTANT SIDE NOTE: Everything just said above is meant to apply only to news *reporters*, not to news *columnists*, *commentators* or *analysts*. The former get paid to not bring their opinions into their work; the latter don't get paid unless they bring their opinions into their work. Sean Hannity on the right and Rachel Maddow on the left, for example, are not "biased journalists." Nor are the distinct ideological bents that come from their coverage the result of their working for media outlets that practice what we described above as directed reporting. Hannity and Maddow are professional opinion-sharers employed by traditional news organizations. Their shows and writings, like those of their contemporaries, are phenomenal destinations for making your voice heard — but don't expect them to do anything but agree with you if you agree with them and argue with you if you don't. They are, like all journalists, unable to be objective. They are also, unlike most journalists, not expected to be fair, either.

OK, LET'S TALK ABOUT 'FAKE NEWS'

No discussion of the modern news buffet would be complete without a mention of its version of the plastic desserts used to entice you to eat the real thing: "fake news." The phrase became popularized in the wake of the 2016 election, perhaps most ringingly when President Donald Trump, during an August 14, 2017, press conference, refused to acknowledge, let alone answer, a question from a CNN reporter, cutting him off and shouting him down by yelling, "You're fake news!"[18] But the practice of making up news stories with no basis in fact and passing them off as the real thing to influence public opinion dates back to at least the 13th Century BC. That's when Rameses the Great whipped up a little fake news portraying the Battle of Kadesh as a resounding victory for the Egyptians; he depicted scenes of him smiting his foes during the battle on the walls of nearly all his temples. Just one problem: The treaty between the Egyptians and the Hittites reveals that the battle was actually a stalemate.[19]

An even juicier example comes from the first century BC. That's when the Roman Emperor Octavian focused the power of fake news on his rival Mark Antony, depicting him as a drunkard, a womanizer and a puppet of the Egyptian queen Cleopatra VII.[20] He even published a document claiming Antony, after he died, wanted to be entombed in the mausoleum of the Ptolemaic pharaohs. That bordered on heresy to the people of Rome—who were so outraged that Antony became a pariah. He eventually killed himself.

Fake news, even though it took awhile for it to become fashionable to call it that, remained a staple of political, ideological and cultural skirmishes through the centuries. George Washington was dogged for decades by letters falsely attributed to him bemoaning how the Revolutionary War was a bad idea and a lost cause.[21] Newspaper magnate William Randolph Hearst effectively started the Spanish-American War with a baldly untrue drawing of Cuban officials strip-searching American women.[22] Emails bounced around the web for more than a decade claiming that atheists were trying to get

Touched by an Angel banned from TV because of its frequent mentions of God — long after the show itself ended and the purported champion of the campaign, Madalyn Murray O'Hair, had gone missing and was presumed dead.[23]

So, fake news by lots of other names was already a fixture in the mediasphere long before Donald Trump's "ties to Russia" and Hillary Clinton's "email servers" were dominating headlines. The rise of social media use over the last decade has unquestionably made fake news easier to spread, meaning it's here to stay as a means some people will use to sway others' thinking on important matters — maybe even matters in your wheelhouse of expertise. That's the bad news. The good news is that the same rise in the use of social media makes such lies easier to spot and debunk. That would be even better news if more people took the time to investigate the truth of things they post before repeating them.

Lest you think, though, as our president and millions of others who both oppose and support him do, that all news you disagree with is "fake," I've cobbled together a handy chart to help you diagnose the kinds of stories, and the reporters who bake them, you're going to encounter at the news buffet. The graphic below charts these on two axes — the inherent fairness or bias of the individual journalist and of the institutional outlet. The four types of resulting outcomes are:

- *Fair individual / fair institution.* This is the quadrant where the vast majority of journalists (except columnists, commentators and analysts, as noted earlier) will fall. The reporter has opinions just like anyone else, but because of his or her professional integrity and his or her employer's status as a legitimate news organization (be it local or national, TV, audio, print or digital), that personal bias doesn't make it into the work product.

- *Fair individual / biased institution.* Here's where you'll find the journalists who work for outlets that practice "directed reporting." A prime example is a news show like *The 700 Club*, produced by the Christian Broadcasting Network (CBN.) The reporters and producers are experienced pros who know how to put a story together. They will ask you questions, only report what you say, not quote you out of context (on purpose.) But their stories will always serve a higher agenda—in this case, spotlighting the goodness and teachings of God—and they aren't shy about it.

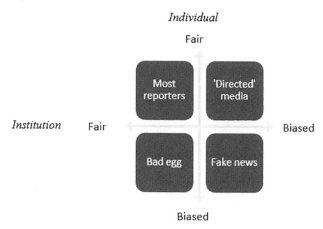

- *Biased individual / fair institution.* You got a bad egg for a storyteller if you wind up in a story that falls in this quadrant. All those things we discussed earlier about suppressing personal opinion and bias in service to the more noble goal of lensless journalism is lost on this individual even though it is expected from his or her employer. Chances are, he or she won't last long drawing a paycheck as a reporter.

- *Biased individual / biased institution.* Prototypical fake news. It's probably a made-up news outlet, designed to mimic a real, trusted source. There is no "reporter" to speak of—just somebody producing a fiction designed to advance an agenda those who've drawn it up want you never to discover. The goal of those who produce items in this quadrant is to make you think they are items in the first quadrant. But now that you've finished this chapter, you're too smart for that, aren't you?

NEXT UP

So far we've talked about the importance of PR as a means to help you translate what's in your heart into a message that changes people's hearts. We've looked at the realities of the news environment in which you want to unleash your message—it most definitely is not what the entertainment industry, or even some of those news outlets themselves, have led you to believe. Now let's pivot from talking about factors external, though critical, to your success in wisely leveraging the expectations and opportunities you find when you sidle up to the news buffet ... and dig in to exactly what you want to say and what you need to do to say it effectively and efficiently. Step 1: Honest and thoughtful assessment of what you offer that your first audience (the media) and their audience (the masses) are going to want to hear and act on.

3

What Do You Bring to the Table, and Who Wants to Eat It?

It's one of the most exhilarating moments in a football game. Team A's offense has been driving the ball down the field for several minutes and now stands just a yard or two from the goal line. They break the huddle and walk to the line of scrimmage, the quarterback surveying the field as he slides up under center, hoping to spot a last-minute weakness in the defense he can exploit for the touchdown.

On the other side of the ball, Team B's defenders are digging in. Literally. Three-hundred-plus-pound linemen kick at the grass and dirt, trying to establish a foothold that will allow them the thrust they'll need off the snap to sack the quarterback or force him to make an errant pass, to tackle the running back for a loss. Other defenders flood the end zone, operating on a field compressed by how close Team A is to paydirt. They don't have the ball, but they want it—or at least they want to keep any of the receivers who will soon be running around with them in the end zone from getting it. The guys in the broadcast booth may like to prattle on about how it's the offense that dictates scoring, but all 11 men on Team B's defense believe the power to add points truly rests with them.

And thus concludes Chapter 3's first lesson in the X's and O's of PR.

You are Team A. The media is Team B. The people you want to reach are the end zone. That's where you want to end up—getting to that audience is how you "score points" with your message. But to get there, you have to go through the press. As we discussed last chapter, most of them will not come after you like a linebacker hell-bent on your destruction. But the fact remains: Just as there is no way for an offense to rack up points on the gridiron without getting the ball past the defense, there is no way for you to score PR touchdowns without drawing up and executing plays that get you past the press and to their viewers, listeners and readers.

Toss my cute sporting metaphor aside if it helps and think of it like this: You have two audiences for your message—the press and the people. You want the first to think you're interesting enough to let you use their megaphone to reach the second. You want the second to engage with you beyond just reading or hearing your words. You can only do either by knowing who you are and what you offer, then spotlighting the aspects of it that will most effectively persuade each audience.

> **You have two audiences for your message— the press and the people. You want the first to think you're interesting enough to let you use their megaphone to reach the second. You want the second to engage with you beyond just reading or hearing your words.**

A BRAND NEW YOU

We've already established you are an author, expert, speaker, coach and/or consultant—that's why you're reading this book. And that you are a bookable spokesperson, a media personality in the making. You are also, as we'll explore in some depth here, a brand. Yep. Just like Starbucks and General Mills and Hilton and Disney and the NFL, you represent a set of values and assets. Those are the distinctives you'll need to lead with in your march toward the goal line of securing meaningful media coverage.

No, this does not mean you need a logo—although you may have one for the services you offer or the business you run. A logo is not your brand—it is a representation of it. A brand goes deeper and wider; it is both the essence and the essentials of what you want to be known for. You have to act, look and sound in a way that reinforces those perceptions. Because, the branding experts will tell you, one negative impression wipes out 10 positive ones. Go "off brand," to use the jargon, and you haven't just taken a few steps back from the end zone, you've been hit with a penalty that costs you 15 yards.

During my time at Focus on the Family, we undertook a massive rebranding campaign designed to, well, refocus our energies and efforts on how we wanted to be known, both to those who used our services and the media who reported about us. Please understand, "rebranding" in this case, and in most cases, doesn't mean drastically changing who you are. Before we started, under the guidance of a crackerjack branding firm (still slaying identity dragons as Signal.csk Brand Partners and still run by Cheryl Farr, who I am blessed to still number among my friends years after we worked together), we were a Christian ministry that offered assistance to families in raising their children, navigating their marriages and walking out their faith in the public square with boldness. That's precisely who we still were when the year-long process ended. What changed was what aspects of our work

Did somebody mention logos? Here's ROAR's, designed to suggest the fierceness with which we work with clients to make sure they make news that matters. And if we blow the other guy's hair back in the process, bravo.

we spotlighted, how we talked about those products and services, and the posture we took in dispensing the advice we continued to dispense to millions of families around the world.

Our challenge was, as discussed in the introduction, positioning the organization favorably to a new generation of families. Our founder, the noted psychologist Dr. James Dobson, was leaving after more than 30 years. His successor, that motorcycle madman Jim Daly, needed to overlay his strengths and experiences on the ministry. Dr. Dobson was an academic with clinical insight into why teenagers rebelled and how to correct it; Jim was a dad whose own two boys were not even teenagers yet. Jim had to advise families from beside them, not from behind a desk or lectern.

Similarly, Dr. Dobson was a major player in conservative public-policy advocacy. Fighting for laws he believed helped families and against those he believed hurt them energized him. He could shut down the Capitol switchboard in minutes by urging his millions of radio listeners to call their congressmen and senators to support or oppose a bill. Jim could have done that, too, but he was not the policy wonk our founder was. He would tackle the issues of Washington, DC, when they rose to a level of urgency, but he was far more passionate about bringing new vigor to the things we did that helped families thrive.

In the end, "Helping families thrive" became Focus on the Family's brand promise under Jim Daly, a departure from "Nurturing and defending families worldwide"—what it had been during Dr. Dobson's final years as the chief voice and face of the organization. Those new words reflected some shifts in optic and operational emphasis: Jim was a next-generation evangelical leader, younger and more vibrant, the kind of husband and father who still romanced his wife and played ball with his kids. He didn't have all the answers, but had to figure them out through applying best practices, so the people he helped would look *to* him as a friend, not *up to* him as an expert and authority. He was not a politics junkie—he cared about what was going on in the halls of power but wasn't much interested in walking them.

Each of these new brand realities had a PR corollary it was my job to leverage. That's why I pushed the crashed-his-Harley-in-the-mountains story, why I forbade Jim from ever wearing a tie on TV again and, in fact, sent a member of my team out to buy him more jeans and sweaters for photo shoots. It's why he never dispensed marriage or parenting tips without indicating he was following them himself as he navigated his own marriage and raised his own children. And it's why he wasn't, as Dr. Dobson had been, the organization's top spokesman for its public-policy advocacy. We even changed the name of the affiliated group through which most of that advocacy was done from Focus on the Family Action to CitizenLink, in order to—as I told the local media—"clarify the identities and the missions of both organizations."[24]

I don't have the $100 million-plus budget of a global organization behind me anymore, with the means to spend hundreds of thousands on 12 months of branding identification and implementation. But, frankly, I don't need it. I can help you harness the high points of your brand and spotlight what differentiates you from your competition in a couple of phone calls or sit-downs. Don't take that to mean it's not intense and intensive work; it is. But it doesn't require a six-figure check or the length of a football season to complete. It is some of the most important work I do in helping clients learn how to—are you sick of this yet? Because I'm not—wisely leverage expectations and opportunities in order to be heard. The fancy textbook term for it is "drafting a value proposition." I prefer talking about it as creating the dough from which we can bake all sorts of cookies to serve at the news buffet. It's where the work truly begins to ensure you properly position your expertise and skills in ways that will persuade the media to book you and their audience to take an interest in you beyond those bookings.

HAVE I GOT A PROPOSITION FOR YOU

Type "value proposition" into Google and you'll find—well, I just did it, on November 10, 2017, and got 7,860,000 results. That's a lot of discussion of the concept, explanations of what they are, examples of good and bad ones and tips on how to create one. *Webster's Dictionary* defines the term as "a statement about the value a product/service might have for a customer."[25] The more highbrow *Cambridge Dictionary* says it's "a reason given by a seller for buying their particular product or service, based on the value it offers customers."[26] These make good bookend definitions for our purposes, because they hint at the slightly different uses of a value proposition in persuading the media and the masses. You want the press to know what they *might miss out on* if they don't engage you; you want the people to know what they *will benefit from* if they do engage you. The value propositions I work with my clients to develop illustrate how they:

1. address real needs for real people (establishing cultural and marketplace relevance)
2. offer specific advantages (pinpointing tangible value)
3. deliver 1 and 2 with peerless expertise and authority (spotlighting the unique credibility of the individual/organization)

This is the perfect time to talk about the PR word I detest the most: spin. It is used, lazily and glibly, to paint as inaccurate and/or insincere statements made by public-relations professionals like me or authors, experts, speakers, coaches and consultants like you. Is it a tactic some in those above groups employ when trying to obfuscate and dodge an unflattering truth? Of course. But those who stoop to it in my profession are the ambulance chasers of the art—sleazy and hopefully not carrying business cards for long that identify them as being in the PR game. As for you and your brethren, when something you say is labeled spin, the labeler is saying you're lying—without having the guts to say you're lying. He or she is hoping the nasty connotations of the word do all his or her dirty work and you are marginalized.

And what are those nasty connotations? Here's the definition as supplied by *Wikipedia*—the only time I'll cite *Wikipedia* in these pages because it is not a serious or authoritative source. I only use

BE CAREFUL WHAT YOU BRAND FOR

As long as we're talking about understanding and advancing your personal brand as an author, expert, speaker, coach or consultant, let's look at the worst branding ever. Or as I like to overdramatically call it: Worst. Branding. Ever.

Words are the first battleground in what used to be called the "culture war" between groups and individuals on opposite sides of the ideological aisle. Those who oppose abortion want to be called "pro-life"; those who wish it to remain legal want to be called "pro-choice." But in the battle for hearts and minds in their public-policy face-offs, they wisely label each other "anti-abortion" and "pro-abortion."

In most cases, conservatives and liberals alike do a good job of not acquiescing to the branding preferences of the other guy. Except—and it's a big except—when it comes to the way those on the right refer to the media they believe lean too far to the left.

They call them the "mainstream media."

You would be hard-pressed to find a more neon-lit example of war-of-words failure in contemporary political discourse. By calling the media they criticize "mainstream," conservatives are voluntarily conveying that they, in fact, are outside of that mainstream. They are branding themselves as fringe—all the more unpardonable because they came up with the word themselves. The media never calls itself "mainstream."

Some Christian conservatives, whether it's because they realize the above or not, prefer instead to refer to the "secular media"—but that's only marginally better. Most people have no idea what "secular" means. Don't believe me? Go out in the street and ask the first 10 people you see to define it for you. And even those who do get it may not think it's a bad thing that the media is not "religious."

So, what—to borrow a phrase from that noted wordsmithing Jedi, Frank Luntz—are words that work in this case? Both "elite media" and "big media" are winners. The first suggests smug prigs like Frasier Crane looking down their noses at the little people, and the latter ... well, nobody likes anything "big"—from Big Brother to big oil to big government—because it carries a whiff of insidiousness.

Those are the terms conservatives ought to be making mainstream.

it now because "spin" doesn't deserve a definition from a serious or authoritative source. "'(S)pin' is a form of propaganda, achieved through providing a biased interpretation of an event or campaigning to persuade public opinion in favor or against some organization or public figure," *Wikipedia* drones. "While traditional public relations and advertising may also rely on altering the presentation of the facts, 'spin' often implies the use of disingenuous, deceptive, and highly manipulative tactics."[27]

So if the language of PR isn't spin, what is it? What are we doing when we create a value proposition that positions us and our services in a way that draws others to us? When we talk about what we do and how we do it with an eye toward getting others to heed us or hire us, what do we call it? Well, one good word is a couple of sentences up. We are *positioning* ourselves advantageously, encapsulating and presenting our brand in a way that emphasizes our authority, insight, expertise, compassion, wisdom or anything else we want to spotlight to create a favorable impression of ourselves. We are not spinning or lying; we are not trying to pass ourselves off as Batman, as popular social media memes urge us, just to make our audience think we're some sort of superhero. We're simply and succinctly putting our best reputational foot forward by using our best rhetorical skills. We are *framing*.

That's the word to remember every time you place your brand before the masses. Framing is the artful positioning of thoughts, actions and results to build the greatest affinity and authority with an audience. "Build" may be the most important word in that definition, because proper framing really is a construction process—the word itself comes from construction, meaning to fit together pieces to give a structure support and shape.[28]

> **Framing is the artful positioning of thoughts, actions and results to build the greatest affinity and authority with an audience.**

That is precisely what we're doing when we do anything well in PR—including creating a value proposition.

My dear friend Jessica Stollings, founder and president of a groundbreaking organization called ReGenerations, hired me to lead her through a value proposition exploration more than five years into her journey as an author, expert, speaker, coach and consultant. ReGenerations (Re-Generations.org) is about not just leveling the walls that divide generations in the workplace and other relational settings, but building bridges across what were once chasms. She wanted to take a fresh look, now that she had a little experiential road behind her, at the *cultural and marketplace relevance* offered by the organization. She wanted to be sure she was consistently communicating the myriad ways in which she *pinpointed tangible value* that *spotlighted the unique credibility* of ReGenerations as an organization and herself as its president.

So where did we begin? We teased out the inputs that fueled her work—such serious issues as generational conflicts, miscommunication between colleagues of different ages, unspoken needs and expectations that hamper productivity. Then we talked through the desired outputs of her clients—increased productivity, clearer communication, greater respect and camaraderie, informed humility and practiced honor. Getting from input to output—or, if you prefer, problem to solution—is the *raison d'etre* of ReGenerations. Our task was to identify, quantify and effectively frame those distinctives for Jessica's potential customers—in the media and in the marketplace.

After a few brainstorming sessions, we translated our thoughts into a fairly standard value proposition format: arresting headline, a paragraph of fuller explanation and three to five bullet points pinpointing the specific advantages of engaging ReGenerations. Returning to my earlier "ball of clay" analogy, I offered Jessica plenty of raw material to choose from.

Headlines

- ReEnergize your team.
- Generate unity. Invigorate people.
- Build bridges across generations.
- Unite generations. Ignite opportunities.
- Team-building solutions for the ages.
- A new org structure for the ages.
- Organizational efficiency for the ages.

Paragraphs

- Harness the unique talents, experiences and passions of your people by connecting emerging generations to established generations in ways that increase productivity, deepen communication, enhance camaraderie and strengthen the bottom line.
- How do you get millennials and Gen X'ers, Baby Boomers and Gen Y'ers, to pursue your company goals cooperatively and effectively? By identifying and harnessing their unique talents, experiences and passions in ways that deepen communication and strengthen the bottom line.
- The modern workplace is a generational soup—millennials and Baby Boomers and Gen X'ers and Gen Y'ers all swimming around together in the broth, trying to help your business achieve its goals. Help them help you by identifying and harnessing their unique talents, experiences and passions in ways that enhance camaraderie and increase productivity.

Bullet points

Tailor-made strategies for:

- Understanding the unique needs, strengths and challenges of every generation
- Identifying and resolving intergenerational conflict
- Leveraging mentoring—from older to younger and vice versa

- Coaching leaders to get maximum results from staff of all experience levels
- Devising policies and procedures that motivate employees of all ages
- Understanding the unique needs, strengths, and challenges of every generation

Good stuff, we thought. But not all the way there. So we talked in detail about the denotative and connotative power of the words and phrases we were using. We bounced ideas and insights off each other about how to go from, to borrow a popular phrase from the business world, good to great. We really liked one headline above all others. But we wanted to play with some thematic content for the paragraph—the idea of the generational mix in the workplace and social scenarios being rich with color and the kindling to truly ignite something special.

We roughed up a Round 2—but still weren't satisfied. Jessica in particular thought we might be complicating things the second time around by trying to be too metaphorical. Conveying the depth and breadth of value can be most powerful and evocative when it's most simple, she decided. So we landed here:

Unite generations. Ignite opportunities.

With 10,000 Baby Boomers retiring each day and Millennials poised to make up half the workforce by 2020, a major demographic shift is under way in America—and in your organization.

It affects every aspect of your business and is ripe with conflict and risk. To succeed moving forward you must develop "generational fluency" to identify and harness the unique talents, experiences and passions of all members of your team in ways that deepen communication, increase productivity and strengthen the bottom line.

Tailor-made strategies for:

- Understanding the needs, strengths and challenges of every generation.
- Leveraging generational differences to build efficient, effective teams that grow stronger over time.
- Embracing mentoring—from older to younger and vice versa.
- Coaching leaders to get maximum results from staff of all experience levels.
- Devising systems and structures that motivate employees, customers and audiences of all ages.

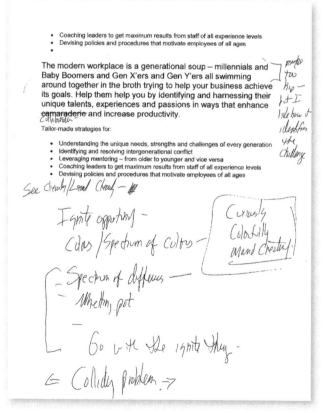

One page of the actual notes from Draft 1 of ReGenerations' value proposition.
Please excuse my doctor-writing-a-prescription handwriting.

And with that, a value proposition was born. In it are elements that can be leveraged and framed to hit either of the two audiences necessary to make news that matters. Business journalists looking for insight into why corporate productivity has stagnated will want to talk to Jessica because she can offer them insights that go beyond the bottom line to the front lines. She can address for them the dysfunctions that infect businesses when Baby Boomers and Gen X'ers and Millennials, the demographic groups that comprise most workforces, can't see eye-to-eye or work hand-in-hand. She sees a problem others don't, and can unpack it for readers/viewers/listeners in ways others can't. But the stories she inhabits, as we've discussed, tell just half the tale. The people she wants to reach, those who will hire ReGenerations to speak to, consult with and coach their employees, are on the other end of those stories. They're the end zone she wants and needs to reach—the ones for whom this problem isn't a theory, but a reality. They need her to provide them with the action points identified in the bullet points.

One more important note from the value proposition Jessica and I created for ReGenerations. You'll notice a phrase in it—a couple of words we both fell in love with: "Generational fluency." That's often the byproduct of deep thinking about your cultural and marketplace relevance that pinpoints your tangible value and spotlights your unique credibility. You hit upon the perfect couple-of-words summation—a verbal calling card. For another of my clients, who writes, speaks and coaches about the hardwired characteristics that govern our makeup far beyond mere personality, the "aha" moment was when we realized he was a "human performance whisperer." For a client whose business helps millionaires cut their tax bills in half, we distilled his value down to "helping the generous become more generous"—giving those with the means to give to charity the opportunity to give more to charity. What do you imagine your pith-perfect—that's not a typo—phrase might be?

I've spent some time on the nitty and the gritty of this exercise Jessica and I undertook to stress that building a value proposition is not something you knock off in an afternoon. Framing your brand is far too critical an assignment for you not to spend the effort and intellect to ensure every word conveys the essence of the attributes and offerings you're carrying into the marketplace of ideas. But it's also important to acknowledge this isn't an exercise in which we're writing in quick-dry cement with our fingers. Value propositions are meant to be living, breathing documents that can change over time as you continue to refine your aspirations as an author, expert, speaker, coach or consultant. What matters most is that you practice the discipline of putting concentrated thought into the words you use to frame your distinctives to the audiences, in the media and the marketplace, you want to reach. Like a football team that wants to score a touchdown, you need to put in the time to draw up the plays that will get you to paydirt. To do anything less will hamstring your ability to make news that matters.

NEXT UP

There's an old journalism saw that says every story must have the five W's and one H: who, what, where, when, why and how. With journalism and PR so closely connected, I'd argue the same applies to a winning public-relations effort. We've just explored how to arrive at your "Who"—understand you're a brand and embrace the process of articulating and framing that brand in a way that will attract media that, in turn, will help you attract influence that, in turn, will help you effect change and engage clients. "What," "Where" and "Why" got their due in earlier chapters. That leaves us "When" and "How." The first of those doesn't need a full chapter—unless I wrote one whose entire content was "Now." So we'll spend our remaining time together on "How." It begins with manufacturing (and I use that word very intentionally) the best possible environment and infrastructure to ensure you are regularly creating opportunities to—a-one, a-two, a-three!—wisely leverage expectations and opportunities in the media to get your message out to the masses. I've got the blueprint … let's grab our PR tool belts and hardhats and get to building our dog-biting machine!

4

If You Build It, They Will Come ... Back

Let's pause in the middle of all this book reading and play a game. Think of your favorite athlete or musician, the man or woman whose exploits on the field or in the recording studio transfix you. On the athlete side, maybe he's a football player with a rifle arm and a heady approach, a quarterback with a knack for winning in the final seconds. Or maybe she's a basketball player with a picture-perfect fadeaway, whose drop step gets her inside the paint faster than anyone you've ever seen on the court. It could be an MMA fighter with power, a gymnast with grace, an archer with pinpoint accuracy, a sprinter with an otherworldly burst out of the blocks.

On the musician side, maybe he's the lead singer of your favorite classic rock band, a vocalist who moves you whether he's crooning a ballad or blasting out a rocker. Maybe she's a folksinger whose lyrics and ethereal voice cut you to the emotional quick, making you see and understand life in ways that enhance it. It could be a drummer with flair, a bassist with bounce, a violinist with perfect pitch, a jazz trumpeter whose name is Miles Davis.

Whoever you're thinking of is almost certainly unique in his or her field, someone with that special something that stretches talent into superstardom. Still, no matter the name in your head, I can tell you one thing about him or her that will be true of anybody else any other reader is thinking about at this same moment. Golfer or guitarist, tennis player or tenor, backup catcher or backup singer, they all have one thing in common: Somebody coached them. Usually formally, in team sports; or in academics, where the coach maybe went by "teacher" instead. In some cases, though, the coach's role was filled by a mentor, trainer or veteran colleague with decades of experience in fill-in-name-of-pursuit-here. And—here's the sentence you ought to underline if you're the underlining type—it is a near surety that while wisdom was being transferred inside the lines and on the stage, support was being given outside them and off it. Success doesn't happen, and can't be sustained, without both. Coaching + Care = Accomplishment.

Consider Michael Jordan, arguably the best player in NBA history, who won six championships with the Chicago Bulls. He wasn't the No. 1 pick in the draft the year he left college—Jordan was selected No. 3, after Akeem (later Hakeem) Olajuwon (who went on to join Jordan as a Hall of Famer) and Sam Bowie (who went on to play forgettably for three teams and be labeled one of the biggest busts in NBA draft history.) But what Jordan lacked in hype coming out of the University of North Carolina he more than made up for not just in skills, but savvy. His coach, the legendary Dean Smith, sharpened the first and taught him the second. So close was their bond that when Smith passed away in 2017, Jordan called him "more than a coach. He was my mentor, my teacher … Coach was always there for me whenever I needed him and I loved him for it. In teaching me the game of basketball, he taught me about life."[29]

You don't have to look far to find similar stories. Serena Williams, the greatest women's tennis player of her generation, credits her coach with taking her from "great to history," guiding her since 2012 to (as of this writing) 10 Grand Slam titles and a pair of Olympic gold medals using methods that transcended just building a better groundstroke.[30] Basketball legend Kareem Abdul-Jabbar wrote in 2017 that he was still learning about his college coach John Wooden and "how deep his influence ran"—more than 50 years after he played for him.[31] Muhammad Ali, the boxer who gave himself the nickname "The Greatest" before he earned it in the ring, talked of his trainer,

Angelo Dundee, as the man who taught him what he needed to thrive inside and outside the squared circle. "He let me be exactly who I wanted to be, and he was loyal," Ali once wrote. "That is the reason I love Angelo."[32]

The value of coaching combined with care to push the coached and cared for to the next level is more than an exercise in anecdotes. Bangor University in Wales conducted a scientific study in 2016 to determine what separates the average Olympic athlete from the superelites who come home with gym bags full of gold medals. The secret ingredients: coaching and care.

"Superelites felt that their coaches fully satisfied their emotional needs by acting as friends, mentors and unwavering supporters—in addition to providing superb technical support," the study found. "High-performing athletes who were not medaled did not feel that way."[33]

"This turns on its head a long-held view that we must simply pair the best technical and tactical coaches to our best athletes to achieve ultimate performance," explained Matthew Barlow, a postdoctoral researcher in sport psychology at Bangor University.[34] Upshot? John Fogerty penned incomplete lyrics to his classic sports anthem "Centerfield." He should have sung, "Put me in coach, *when you think* I'm ready to play."

> **You will need to join the ranks of the coached and cared for to put your best PR foot forward, to be heard in that noisy marketplace of ideas we've been talking about.**

I just spent several paragraphs of the book on this because there's a critical principle here for you, as someone who aspires to be a superelite in—roll tape!—wisely leveraging expectations and opportunities in the media to get your message out to the masses. You will need to join the ranks of the coached and cared for to put your best PR foot forward, to be heard in that noisy marketplace of ideas we've been talking about.

This is not meant to discount your natural abilities. If you're an author, you can obviously write. If you're a public speaker, you can obviously hold an audience's attention. I have no doubt there is all variety of raw talent roiling around inside you that will help you make your mark on the media. But it needs to be harnessed, shaped, directed, trained, steeped in the expertise of others who have already spent years in the arena you want to walk into. There simply is no other path to strategically crafted and applied public relations that consistently lays a good bite into a dog.

I speak this truth from experience. I was coached, not educated, into my journalism career, which I then flipped into my PR career. My college degree is in neither discipline, but in English—as much in literature as in the compositional arts. Everything I know I learned on the job from mentors who took me under their wing to teach me what they knew, then pat me on the back when I got it right and pick me up when I didn't. Sure, I had natural ability. I'd been writing since I was a kid—tapping out scripts about supercops for my school buddies and me to star in all the way back to fifth grade. But my raw talents needed to be harnessed and directed, seasoned with the experience of others who'd actually solved crimes with their reporting and writing, before I could honestly wear the mantle of "journalist." And it was only after 15 years of doing so, crossing paths daily with scores of professionals (locally and nationally) whose jobs were to convince me to write about their clients, that I learned enough to switch sides and earn a living doing it myself. My journey from the persuaded to the persuader was only possible, and then successful, because of their coaching and care.

CAMPAIGNING AGAINST CAMPAIGNS

When the authors, experts, speakers, coaches and consultants I work with honor me by bringing me aboard as their PR coach, Job 1 is not, as many might expect, to set in motion a campaign touting a newsworthy aspect of their brand. Highlighters ready? Start underlining: Your goal at the outset of stepping into the mediasphere is not to launch a PR campaign, because campaigns end; good, effective PR never does. It's the difference between paving a road and erecting a city. Writing a speech and creating a language. Going for a walk and learning to walk. Unleashing the power of PR to make news that matters—to leverage endless opportunities to bite the dog—requires more thought initially than action. You don't need to build interest—not yet. You need to build infrastructure. That's the superhighway to becoming superelite.

Let's examine what form this takes by considering the case of NÜRESH (nuresh.com), a revolutionary mobile and digital platform that allows users to—as President Steve Reiter and I articulated in the company's value proposition—stream their way to personal development. NÜRESH—also from the value prop—gives subscribers thousands of hours of the most inspirational and informative premium spoken-word content in one innovative and easy-to-use Web interface. It allows them to listen, learn and still have time to live life. Before I did a nanosecond of work for Steve as his coach, I proposed these steps to get NÜRESH's PR infrastructure up and operational.

> **Your goal at the outset of your foray into the mediasphere is not to launch a PR campaign, because campaigns end; good, effective PR never does. You don't need to build interest— not yet. You need to build infrastructure.**

1. NÜRESH 101: ROAR needs to "go to school" on NÜRESH, intellectually downloading the anecdotal history, technical specs, contributor roster and strategy, and service operating and expansion goals. This will be used to create materials and to assess media potential.

2. Press Kit/Web Content Creation: It is important to note that the first instances of execution will not likely involve robust numbers of appearances and/or publication. The first PR impression NÜRESH will make is on its website and in the language describing it in app stores. It is essential this material is crafted with the proper branding to position the service as the unique, user-friendly, content-rich experience it is. ROAR will create this content, including:

- All website verbiage (About Us, How it Works, etc.)
- Service value proposition
- Company bios / Edits to contributor bios for consistency in the platform, as needed

3. Infrastructure must be created and paired with the ongoing discipline of assessing news trends and daily news events with the singular purpose of identifying and creating opportunities for NÜRESH to be sought after by news organizations. We want to attract them to the service and value it provides and by extension, be heard by their audiences across media type and niche. We want to be making news and be quoted when news is made in the areas where the brand and value proposition reach.

4. Media training: We will educate organizational voices in the art of the interview—from developing talking points and winsomely sticking to them no matter the direction the questioning goes to presentation tips depending on the type of media being engaged. We will offer real-time and ongoing feedback and ample opportunities for consistent practice.

There is no one-size-fits-all blueprint for building a PR infrastructure. While the steps above follow a pretty standard progression whether I'm working with a pastor or a pasta maker, the details are always specific to the value offered and the goals being pursued by the author, expert, speaker, coach or consultant. This is a custom, not a cookie-cutter, build.

HE WHO REPRESENTS HIMSELF HAS A FOOL FOR A (PR) CLIENT

Disclaimer: This is not a sales pitch. It's a serious plea. It's also an essential—nonnegotiable, really—part of building an effective PR infrastructure: Having someone who serves as your publicist, even if you don't hire someone to serve as your PR coach/director.

That's because you never, ever, under any circumstance, no matter how friendly you think they are, even if you went to school or belong to a club with them, you can't think of a reason that would make me change my mind, allow a journalist direct access to you.

Interviews are serious business—as we've discussed. To do your best, you need to know what the reporter's piece is about, what perspective he or she wants you to provide. You must make sure you're not serving the journalist's agenda, but yours. What project or passion do you want to talk about regardless of the questions posed to you? You can't accomplish that if a reporter can ring you up and launch into Q-and-A mode.

I've seen careers ruined because reporters called or dropped in on talent directly—prompting rushed, stumbling responses (not even always in crisis-management situations) that never would have been uttered had the subject been able to think through and reasonably frame what he or she wanted to say. If ever a reporter does find a way to get to you directly, always have a PR person you can send him or her to in order to give yourself that all-important preparation time.

Bottom line: If you're big enough that the press wants to talk to you on a regular basis, be smart enough to engage the services of folks like us to ensure your best interests are served.

That said, there are a few universals I place into every build-out of every plan—sort of like having bathrooms in a house. It's not a functional structure without them. First is something you should not even wait to finish reading beyond this sentence to do: Set up a Google alert for your name, your business's name and the key words and phrases that describe the services you offer.

STAYING ALERT

Google alerts are a wonderful, and free, subscription service of sorts that let you know when the media is talking about you or what you do. Setting them up is easy; follow the instructions here: google.com/alerts. Be careful what you ask to be alerted to, though, he adds, getting all coachy on you. If you're a pastor, asking for an email every time "God" shows up in the news is a recipe for gigabytes of irrelevant notices. If you're a pasta maker, typing "spaghetti" into the system will net you the same thing. The best place from which to pull search terms, actually, is your value proposition—especially the bullet points. If you haven't finished that exercise yet, look at the assets you do have—and lift the words most focused on the uniqueness of the services and/or products you offer. If you find yourself getting alerts that play like spam, you can always adjust for more specificity later.

What's the value, you may be wisely asking, of learning about news stories done on your areas of insight and expertise after they've already been published and broadcast? By then, hasn't the boat already floated? Yes and no. It is highly unlikely a news outlet will turn around a day or two after producing a story on a topic ideally suited to you and repeat itself. But for stories that appear online and/or in print, you do have an immediate opportunity: the good old-fashioned letter to the editor. Yes, you're going to have limited space—few publications allow letters of more than 300 words, and many won't accept anything more than half that. But it is a chance for you to add your pair of pennies to a discussion in your neighborhood of the mediasphere. More important, it is, by far, the lowest-hanging fruit available for plucking when it comes to getting into the press and being seen by their audiences. Can you really *roar* in a letter to the editor? That's tough. But even a whisper means you're being heard.

That brings us to another bit of standard equipment in any PR infrastructure I help a client—sorry, "superelite in training"—build. Think of it as living to fight another day. It involves reaching out to the reporter of the story you wished you had been in and doing what it takes to get in his or her Rolodex/smartphone contact list. Compliment the piece. Offer to send your book or product. Add some fresh perspective on the subject covered that will entice him or her to call you back. What you need to know about journalists is that they're always looking for new sources. Sure, they have their favorite go-to's—but every one of them started as a first-timer. Put in the effort to increase your chances of becoming a first-timer, and you've taken a step toward becoming a go-to. I still have one reporter I can shoot a text to, a household face and name I first encountered more than a decade ago at Focus on the Family. He trusted me enough back then that he would get my thoughts about the angles he should pursue for stories we weren't even part of—and just a few weeks prior to me typing these words he helped me get a foot in the door for a client at his millions-of-eyeballs outlet. (Side note: You know if you read the previous PR-verb that I don't mean *you*, personally, should be the one forging these relationships. I mean the universal you. You and your PR pro. You can always pass personal greetings, thanks and appreciation through him or her—but always remember to keep a buffer between you and the press. It not only protects you, as described earlier, it signals to the journalist that you're a legit newsmaker. You have *people*. Seriously, that may sound arrogant, but it helps establish authority and gravitas. In the same way having a gmail.com or yahoo. com email address lessens the professionalism of a businessperson, having a PR representative enhances the reputation of a news source.)

If you really want to practice the art of committing news (the subject of Chapter 6), though, merely responding to mentions of your areas of interest and aptitude won't cut it. Your awareness of the news and information percolating all around you has to be deeper, and far more proactive, if you hope to bite the dog. After all, you can't—been awhile, hasn't it?—wisely leverage the media's expectations and opportunities unless you're aware of what those expectations and opportunities are.

To do that you have to be well-read, well-watched and well-listened. You have to know what's being talked about in the news so you can spot those openings for your message. This is, again, an area in which your PR coach can help you immeasurably. Jump back to my infrastructure blueprint for NÜRESH and you'll see it was point No. 3.

A good example of this for another of ROAR's clients came during the holiday season of 2016, which fell in the wake of Donald Trump's surprising win over Hillary Clinton in the presidential election. Then President-elect Trump was taking Ray-Bradbury-novel levels of heat from the media for being, in a very few

> **You have to be well-read, well-watched and well-listened. You have to know what's being talked about in the news so you can spot those openings for your message.**

of their words, boorish, petty, unqualified, bitter and narcissistic. His response to the tsunami of criticism was to use Twitter, as he'd done throughout the campaign, to lash and bluster back at his detractors. It was shaping up to be a very unmerry Christmas. I hatched an idea in the midst of all this bah humbug for Michael Anthony, a pastor whose ministry distinctive as founder of a group called Godfactor is calling Christians to humility and repentance. The gist was an op-ed titled "Don't Be a Donald This Christmas"—leveraging the Yuletide dispiritedness of the election fallout and Trump's apparently thin skin with the highlights of Michael's value proposition. The ensuing piece endeavored to help everyday Americans get through the customary trials we all face when we gather with friends and family for extended periods of time, in close quarters, to celebrate the Most Wonderful Time of the Year.

Townhall.com, one of the most influential conservative sites on the web, bit on the pitch faster than the British bite into figgy pudding. Michael's essay read in part:

The president-elect's troubles in holding his tongue—and his keyboard—when criticized can actually be instructive to all of us this holiday season. Alec Baldwin may not be launching into an unflattering impersonation of us at the dinner table, but the friends and relatives we will be sharing turkey and mistletoe with can give us a bad case of what I call 'epidermis penetratus'—the ability to get underneath our skin.

Being human means being imperfect—and one of our imperfections is to forget this basic truth. Each of us has caused someone else to have a serious case of epidermis penetratus, too. At times, we all think our way is best, and that everyone else is the problem. If you do this, you're setting yourself up for folly.

It's very easy to forget that each of us have our own idiosyncrasies, mannerisms and faults that will annoy other people. Yes, Mr. Trump, even you. Recognizing this will help humble you so that you can interact with others in ways that simply won't be possible if you merely think everyone else is the problem. If you work on yourself, you just may find that your interactions with others may take less work.[35]

ROAR client Michael Anthony turned a radio interview about then-GOP presidential candidate Donald Trump into a CNN appearance by—let me turn the sound down so I can hear you—wisely leveraging expectations and opportunities. (You Tube screen capture.[36])

Michael deserves all the credit for making this work by immediately catching the vision for the idea and executing it with practical wisdom relayed with tongue-very-near-cheek-if-not-firmly-planted-there. But it never would have happened had we not built the infrastructure that allowed us to assess the news climate and determine where he could fit in. Michael is still utilizing that infrastructure today; we built it, and they keep on coming.

Oh, I almost forgot. His piece had a righteous man-bites-dog aspect to it. Michael is a conservative Christian radio host who had broken a pretty significant story during the campaign about Trump's spiritual journey (which wound up prompting a CNN hit, but that's a tale for a different day.) The press expected from someone with his political pedigree a humorless response to all the barbs the president-elect was taking. We upset their expectations, which is the most effective way to leverage them. We'll explore that in detail next chapter.

Before we move on, let's look quickly at this piece from one more angle. You'll remember back in Chapter 1 we talked about the value of earned media versus paid media, of news stories you don't pay for versus advertising you do. Our conclusion, backed by research and common-sense anecdotal evidence, was that not paying for coverage builds more affinity for you and your thoughts and offerings than paying for spots does. You may recall, though, that I made passing reference to it being possible to put a monetary value on the stories you become part of. Its fancy industry acronym is AVE, or Ad Value Equivalency, and it represents how much you'd have to pay in ad dollars to secure the same coverage you got for nothing because you *earned* it. In the case of Michael's *Townhall.com* piece, that number—as computed by Meltwater Media, one of the industry's top PR software suites—was $17,668.22. It reached an audience of 1.9 million.

Now, Michael has built Godfactor into a relevant organization with a popular blog through which he routinely reaches thousands of loyal readers. But in a single article created through strategically crafted and applied public relations, he reached exponentially more with an impact that paid for itself and then some when you ledger it alongside ROAR's monthly rate.

TOUCHED BY AN ANECDOTE

When you've won nine Emmys, as Mark Burnett has, you can just plop them down on a bookshelf in the house—which is where this Outstanding Reality Competition Program statue wound up for a time in 2013. (Personal photo.)

Roma Downey is an Emmy-nominated actress best known for headlining the hit CBS TV series *Touched by an Angel* for nine seasons. She also played Jackie Kennedy Onassis in the Emmy-winning miniseries *A Woman Named Jackie*. Mark Burnett is the most prolific and successful reality TV producer in history, whose hit shows include *Survivor*, *The Voice*, *Shark Tank*, *The Apprentice* and *The Celebrity Apprentice* (which made him, at one time, our president's boss.) He's won nine Emmys. Most important to them, they are also husband and wife. Between them, they had done hundreds, perhaps even thousands, of interviews by the time I worked with them in 2013.

The couple was poised to release their grandest project yet as production partners, the HISTORY Channel miniseries *The Bible*, when they engaged the firm I worked for to help them spread the word about the 10-part saga covering the greatest stories of Scripture from Genesis to Revelation. But they looked to us for more than access to our contacts in the faith-based press. They wanted us to help them prepare for the interviews they'd be doing with those press—and for the faith-tinged questions they'd be getting from the usual outlets they talked to, from *Good Morning America* to *The Hollywood Reporter*. They wanted us to coach them.

Media training, you'll recall, is one of the pivotal pieces of equipment you'll find in any PR infrastructure. I cite all of Roma's and

Mark's experience in front of cameras, microphones and notebooks not to impress you—but to stress how critical it is you have someone who can, with impartiality and expertise, assess how prepared you are for the questions you'll face and to better prepare you based on your aptitude and need. Put in less touchy-feely terms: If two people with their years and levels of success and experience thought they could benefit from media coaching, you can bet you will, too.

I prepared a thick document filled in part with cues to prompt stories about their reasons for tackling the project, how and why they chose the actors they did for so many iconic roles, interesting things that happened on set, etc. Another large portion of the prep packet was to anticipate and help them think through the deeper and in some cases tougher questions: the thorny finer points of theology, Christian views on public-policy debates, the inevitable asks about their personal faith journeys. The goal here was not, please remember, to *spin* their answers; it was to help them think through and practice what they wanted to say about the project and their involvement in it. We didn't put words in their mouths; we helped them get words out of their heads and hearts.

To that end, we did a couple rounds of mock interviews. I remember one in particular, in the living room of their beautiful cliffside home in Malibu (OK, maybe I was trying to impress you just a *little bit* there ☺.) I was playing the role of hostile interviewer, seeing if I could knock them off stride, to unnerve them enough to follow my agenda and not pursue their own. I turned to Mark, seated in an overstuffed leather chair just a few feet to my left, and asked, barely concealing a sneer: "Why did you, of all people, make a miniseries called *The Bible*? I mean, you're Mr. Vote 'Em Off the Island. Now people are supposed to take you seriously as preacher of the Word of God?" Mark paused. I got him, I thought. But the pause was only to collect his emotions as he explained that he wasn't looking to preach to anybody. That, he explained, was the church's job. He was just a filmmaker and a Christian who wanted to unite those dual passions. His emotion was palpable as he explained how the Bible that informed *The Bible* meant so much to him and his wife that they hoped their series would lead others to pick up the book and explore its wonders for themselves. It was a powerful, authentic response and, yes, it had some man-bites-dog in it: The King of Reality TV, the ultimate Hollywood powerbroker, has to settle himself when talking about his love for God. Expectations, leveraged.

Actor Diogo Morgado, who played Jesus in Roma Downey's and Mark Burnett's miniseries *The Bible*, was dubbed #HotJesus by fans on social media. The PR guy with him has never been dubbed hot anything by anybody. (Personal photo.)

I also did some media training with Diogo Morgado, the young actor who played the lynchpin role of Jesus. Preparing him was more a matter of making him comfortable talking about faith topics with faith press. Diogo is Portuguese, a member of a culture that is intensely private about religious matters. I actually discovered a perfect story he could tell without having to talk about personal faith while we were making small talk on a flight to a convention. He told me, matter-of-factly really, that when he filmed the scene of Jesus' Crucifixion, which like all film scenes involved a few seconds of action followed by minutes of waiting, repeated in a seemingly endless loop, he closed his eyes to rest as the minutes of inactivity dragged on. It was cold and he was exhausted and he saw in a flash in that moment, he said, images of things he regretted he had done or not done in his life. This time, it was the PR guy who got choked up. I urged Diogo to tell that story often—the power of his experience playing Jesus would, in almost all cases, deter reporters from asking him about his personal faith. They would have their "lead"—the actor who played Jesus sees a vision of his regrets while hanging on the cross.

One more story about the importance of media training: One of Dr. James Dobson's favorite shows to do while he was running Focus on the Family was *Larry King Live*. King was the broadest interviewer working during his heyday—meaning he may not have dug deeply into an issue with two or three follow-up questions, but he would hit you, over the course of an hour, with more queries than any other host. To prepare for a Larry King interview was to prepare for the Spanish Inquisition—if the Spaniards were merely curious rather than bloodthirsty. The prep books my team and I prepared for Dr. Dobson for each booking were dozens of pages thick. If it had been in the news since the last time he and Larry shared that iconic set at CNN's Los Angeles studios, it could come up in the interview. If it was a historical, philosophical or religious point likely to pique Larry's interest, we had to be ready. I used to joke that written on one of Larry's trademark blue cards that he shuffled through every show was the question, "Who was your favorite Catwoman on the 1960s *Batman* TV show?"—and we had to make sure Dr. Dobson said "Julie Newmar" because there is no other right answer.

You know what's funny about all the prep books we did for the half-dozen *Larry King Live* appearances Dr. Dobson made during my time as his PR coach? I can't recall a single instance in which he uttered even one of the talking points we provided. We're talking, conservatively, a couple of reams of paper over five or six years. Tens of thousands of words. And none of them made it from the sheet to Dr. Dobson's brain, out his mouth and onto the air. Why? He was that good. When the red light came on and Larry asked him even the things only Larry would ever ask anybody, Dr. Dobson simply had the answers already in his head. That might lead you to conclude the time spent on all that getting-ready was wasted. You'd be wrong. The prep served a critical purpose for Dr. Dobson even though he never used it to prompt his answers. How so? It made him feel comfortable and confident every time he sat behind Larry's desk. He may have never used the words we gave him, but he most definitely needed them.

No clearer picture can be painted, in the world of public relations, of what it means to be coached and cared for. When the relationship works, you are readied for the worst, so you can do your best. You may know your stuff backwards and forwards, but the coach is there to help you grab hold of the ups and ride out the downs. He or she is confidante, consoler, cajoler. A second set of eyes and ears. The architect of your infrastructure, the one who helps you own the zone of your influence and expertise.

NEXT UP

I just ran a word search on this manuscript and so far I have used some variation of "leverage" 31 times—including that last one right there. We'll explore why in Chapter 5 (hint: It's not because I need a thesaurus.) It's because making news that matters is a whole lot like hand-to-hand combat—at least the kind on display in action classics like *Above the Law, Hard to Kill, Marked for Death* and, of course, *Under Siege*. No, you don't need to be able to beat up a barroom full of bad guys with a cue ball wrapped in a towel or save a nuclear submarine from falling into the nefarious hands of a wildly overacting Tommy Lee Jones. You just need to know when and how to apply the right kind of pressure in the right kind of ways. C'mon, the sensei awaits.

5

Everything I Know About PR
I Learned From Steven Seagal

Detective Gino Felino is a kid from Brooklyn who grew up to patrol his old neighborhood of Dyker Heights—sort of the NYPD's version of *Welcome Back, Kotter.* But Gino's dreams were not his ticket out. He's not trying to teach a lovable group of Sweathogs who just need someone to believe in them. He's trying to clean up the mean streets of his youth after his partner and childhood pal Bobby Lupo is executed gangland style in front of his wife and kids. Gino knows who did it—another old running buddy from back in the day, Richie Madano. But proving it, and bringing the increasingly drug-crazed Richie to justice ... well, that's a different story.

It's the story of *Out for Justice,* Steven Seagal's fourth (three-word-titled) feature film, released in 1991. It is notable for a few things: It was the actor's film just prior to his biggest box office and critical success, *Under Siege,* a year later; it features him affecting an Italian accent so wretched that it might not even be permitted today—not based on lack of artistic merit so much as protests from Italian-Americans who would think it a cultural insult; and, I feel confident in guaranteeing, this book is the only time you will ever see it spotlighted as instructive of how PR works when done right.

We'll skip the rest of the plot—except to note that Gino eventually does dispatch Richie (with a corkscrew to the forehead)—and go right to the most memorable scene. It's a roughly two-minute barroom brawl that was the best example at that time, and may still be the best example in his long and now direct-to-video career, of Seagal's signature martial arts fighting style: aikido.

Gino tosses macho insults and threats at the patrons of Richie's brother Vinnie's bar, trying to smoke out his prey, before finally getting tired of Vinnie insulting him by saying the only thing that makes him a tough guy is his gun and his badge. So Gino unloads and sets down the piece, and offers the shield as the trophy to anyone who can take it from around his neck. Vinnie then announces he'll give $5,000 to the henchman who captures it, and the fight is on.

Bad Guy No. 1 takes a swing at Gino and misses. He falls forward with the momentum of his punch and gets Gino's fist in his face. He collapses in a heap.

Bad Guy No. 2—wearing a slick left-over-from-the-'80s polyester track suit with waves of purple, yellow and blue in it—lunges at Gino next, taking a shot at his head. Gino steps back, grabs his attacker's hand, wraps it in a bar towel he picked up while he was speechifying and uses the towel and Bad Guy No. 2's momentum to flip him over a table.

Gino then pulls from his pocket a cue ball he plucked earlier from the pool table and puts it inside the towel before Bad Guy No. 3 comes at him. He's a tattooed, goateed, mulleted fat dude who flips his central-casting-issued toothpick aside and utters a delightfully over-the-top action-movie quip. He then threatens to cut Gino's $%$#@(& head off and stabs at him with a knife in his right hand. Gino responds by stepping back and aside, pushing Bad Guy No. 3 forward with his left hand and smacking him in the chops with the cue-ball towel with his right.

Bad Guy No. 4 quickly follows, swinging a pool cue like John Henry wielding a steel-drivin' hammer. Gino backs away, and Bad Guy No. 4's momentum after missing causes him to stumble forward. Gino helps him to the floor by whapping him in the back of the head with the cue-ball towel. Bad Guy No. 5—our first henchman in full wife-beater regalia—charges Gino mindlessly, getting slapped in the hand with the cue-ball towel, then back-kicked in the face as his momentum bends him toward Gino's foot. Bad Guy No. 6—or he may be an earlier Bad Guy back in the fray; it's hard to keep track—similarly jumps at Gino without a plan, and winds up flipped over the pool table as Gino gracefully steps aside and pushes him.

Bad Guy No. 3 returns to spit a few teeth Gino knocked loose on the pool table, then swings at our hero. Gino blocks the punch, freezing Bad Guy No. 3 in perfect position to get another wallop with the cue-ball towel. Down goes Frazier.

Enter Bad Guy No. 7—Sticks—who just happens to be sitting in the pool table bleachers carrying lethal-looking martial arts, well, sticks. As Gino prepares to face him, Bad Guy No. 2 re-emerges, sitting up on the floor and cracking Gino across the back of the legs with a pool cue. Gino falls, but gets up in time to meet Bad Guy No. 2 as he surges forward—whipping the cue-ball towel into his face and knocking him back to the floor.

And then Sticks and Gino go at it—Gino with a pool cue. They whip and clack at each other for nearly 30 seconds, Sticks conveniently splitting Gino's cue in half at one point so they can both wave and whipsaw with two sticks apiece. Eventually, Sticks lunges forward with a swipe, and Gino takes a step back, grabs his hand, snaps it backwards and punches him in the face and to the floor.

Here comes Bad Guy No. 8! He runs and swings simultaneously at Gino, who leans away from the punch, grabs his hands and flips him to the ground. Bad Guy No. 9 is up next, having learned nothing from watching his compatriots fail at the running swing. He executes the same maneuver, gets punched in the gut and flipped on the pool table by a backpedaling Gino.

Bad Guy No. 10 at least tries something new: kicking at Gino from atop the pool table. Gino sidesteps the kick, catches his leg, socks him in the crotch and takes advantage of his being off balance by picking up a pool cue—or the piece of one he was using to fight Sticks—and swatting his legs out from under him.

Bad Guy No. 11 is really a reluctant afterthought, backing away scared as Gino shoves him into a phone booth and slams the door shut with him inside. Gino, having vanquished all Vinnie's muscle, then walks up to the man himself. They trade swear words and bad accents, and Gino knocks him bloody and cold with a single shot to the face.

Fini—like they say in all the arthouse films.

You can watch the whole scene on *YouTube* by typing "out for justice pool hall scene" into a Web browser. You'll see far better than I can describe—but it sure was fun trying—the uniqueness of Seagal's fighting style. Hollywood had never witnessed anything like it when he made his film debut in 1988's *Above the Law*. Martial-arts movies up till that time, starring the likes of Bruce Lee and Chuck Norris, featured far more aggressive punches and kicks from their heroes. Hand-and-foot-to-hand-and-foot combat in their movies pitted attackers against attackers, with Lee and Norris winning by being more relentless attackers. Seagal won fights in almost 180-degree fashion, using all the energy his attackers aimed in his direction against them. His power came from leveraging their power, marshaling their momentum to fuel his victory.

"We allow the other person to attack and use his own attack against him by becoming one with his movement and utilizing anatomical weak points, joint blocks and throws, etc.," Seagal once said, explaining the art of aikido in which he is a 7th-dan black belt. "In a life-and-death situation, the harder the technique becomes. Oftentimes, the attacker creates the life-and-death situation, because the harder they come the harder they fall. These techniques will work on anybody, but you really have to learn them," he added. "Aikido is not a quick art to learn."[37]

> **Don't wrap a cue ball in a towel; wrap your value proposition in an offer journalists can't help but fall for when you hit them with it.**

Neither is PR. And it works in pretty much the same way. That mantra we've been repeating since the introduction about public relations being the wise leveraging of expectations and opportunities? Sounds a lot like what Seagal did to that barroom of bad guys in *Out for Justice*, doesn't it? No, that doesn't mean you need to start beating up reporters, even the ones who land a good distance away from BFFs on the scale discussed in Chapter 2. It means you need to be aware of the momentum they're generating with their coverage, the momentum the mediasphere is generating in general, and learn the artful application not of joint blocks and throws, but of news pitches and coverage creation. Don't wrap a cue ball in a towel; wrap your value proposition in an offer journalists can't help but fall for when you hit them with it.

MEET, EXCEED, UPSET

Interestingly enough, I started working in daily journalism a year before Seagal debuted onscreen in *Above the Law*. That makes us contemporaries of a sort. His 30-plus years of experience informs his teaching that the strategy of aikido is all about "blending, moving, leading."[38] Mine informs my telling you the strategy of public relations is all about meeting, exceeding and upsetting. He's talking about leveraging people trying to hit you. I'm referring to leveraging those expectations and opportunities we've been talking so much about.

The lowest-hanging fruit, as discussed prior, is simply to meet opportunities. These are those stories you get quotes in or create that don't quite make it to bite-the-dog territory. They are instead a function of your brand distinctives and expertise aligning with a story already in the news or a trend already in the culture. I call it *carpe headlinum* — seizing the headlines. ROAR client Brad Kullman has had tremendous success in this swatch of the mediasphere. Brad is an author and speaker with an impressive resume that includes nearly 20 years working as a Major League Baseball scout and front-office executive, including a stint as general manager of the Cincinnati Reds. One of Brad's passions is tanking — teams that lose on purpose, or at least don't try to win on purpose, in the hopes of netting higher draft picks today who may become future stars and lead them to championships tomorrow.

Actually, Brad's passion isn't tanking—it's eliminating tanking. It's the goal of his first book, *Losing (To Win): How Incentivized Losing Undermines the Integrity of Our Major Professional Sports Leagues*. He's not the only analyst/commentator/thought leader to hold that opinion, but he is the first to create a solution rooted in something other than fines: reworking the drafts in all four major sports from a reverse-standings model (the worse you are, the higher you pick) to an "integrity-based" model (which rewards teams that continue trying to win even if a championship is out of grasp for the season.) As we crafted it in his value proposition, "Brad Kullman sees a scandal brewing in professional sports today that makes the Black Sox seem like child's play. As entire organizations in the NFL, MLB, NBA and NHL conspire to throw games, selling this fraud to fans, Kullman offers a vision for returning integrity to competition."

Within days of our finishing the value prop exercise, a sports columnist for *The Washington Post* opined that the Green Bay Packers, in the throes of foundering after losing All-World quarterback Aaron Rodgers to a broken collarbone, should tank the season and retool, arguing that since they had no chance to make the playoffs with Rodgers' underperforming understudy under center, they had nothing worthwhile to play for but a higher draft pick. "During Rodgers' tenure, the Packers annually have picked at the bottom of the draft, the one drawback to possessing one of the best quarterbacks in the NFL," *The Post*'s Adam Kilgore wrote. "They can salvage their season without Rodgers through losing not a little, but a lot. They are bad without Rodgers. They should be as bad as possible and tank for the highest draft pick they can get."[39]

Them was fightin' words to the guy with "a bold blueprint for how to put the 'compete' back in major league sports competition" (also from Brad's value proposition.) It created a clear opportunity he was uniquely qualified and prepared to meet—especially since it came mere days after MLB's Houston Astros won the World Series just a few years after tanking their way through three 100-loss seasons. So I reached out personally to a sports editor at *The Post* with a proposal: Let Brad make a case for why tanking-for-titles is not the answer, for the Packers or the Astros or any other team in any other sport, and certainly not for fans. The result? An op-ed on the website of the eighth-largest paper in the US, a piece that allowed Brad to join Woodward and Bernstein as writers whose bylines appeared in *The Washington Post*. His most compelling point was aimed squarely at the fans reading the piece—tailor-made to motivate them to act on his message by buying his book or joining him in advocating for his revolutionary reforms.

His payoff paragraph was crafted to help those fans envision an era when every game at every point in the season was worth watching.

Sports • Perspective

Take it from a former GM: We should not reward tanking. Here's a proposal to end it for good.

By Brad Kullman November 14

Brad Kullman's 2017 op-ed in *The Washington Post* helped establish his authority as the leading voice against tanking-for-titles in pro sports. It also reached a potential audience of more than 39 million and was worth $361,134.81 in Ad Value Equivalency (AVE.)[41]

"The top teams continue jockeying for home-field advantage, just as they are now," Brad wrote.

> But the middle-of-the-pack teams, who may have been eliminated in Week 15 or 16, are still in the thick of it for a top draft pick. The organization will still have every incentive to give all they have to win out, rather than 'shutting down' millionaire superstars based on the manufactured excuse of wanting to 'look at' backups and third-stringers. Even the teams at the bottom of the standings will have incentive to fight to avoid the cellar, since even a single additional victory can easily mean five or 10 spots higher in the draft. Rather than the majority of teams left with 'nothing to play for' in Week 17, the action will be intense across the board, as teams compete for their present, as well as their future.[40]

We weren't done, though. We doubled down on meeting opportunity and created some new ones—putting Brad's piece and the plan behind it in the hands of national and local sports talk show and podcast hosts across the country. That led to a whole new round of media appearances for Brad to make news that mattered, from Portland to Jacksonville to the coast-to-coast coverage of NBC Sports Radio. At each stop, he made disciples and converts to his vision, a key part of his brand strategy of effecting change in the games we love by first starting a grassroots movement, then looking to persuade the leagues and the teams themselves that there is a better way.

Stories that spring from meeting opportunities are stories even if we aren't part of them; those generated by exceeding and upsetting expectations are stories only because we're part of them.

As we—to quote Sensai Seagal—blend, move and lead into the arena of expectations, we enter serious bite-the-dog territory. When we make news here, it's because we *made* news here. We aren't plugging in to an existing narrative; we are creating our own. Stories that spring from meeting opportunities are stories even if we aren't part of them; those generated by exceeding and upsetting expectations are stories only because we're part of them. Dogs are harmed in the creation of news in the latter category—relax, relax, I'm speaking purely metaphorically, only in the communications sense.

Exceeding the expectations of the media to encourage coverage means you say, do or offer something that doesn't surprise them, but you offer it in a way that does. A great generic example of this kind of newsmaking can be found in companies and services in the "doing good" / social-justice philanthropy sector. These are businesses, usually conceived and run by Millennials, like TOMS Shoes (for every pair you buy, a pair is donated to the needy in an undeveloped country), The Giving Keys (a portion of all proceeds go to employing and housing the homeless) and Warby Parker (buy a pair of glasses and a pair is donated to the less fortunate.) They offer desirably trendy products for sale, like any other company trying to carve out lucrative market share, but they don't stop there. They exceed the corporate-profitmaking expectation by supporting charities that serve communities and people in need. That gets TOMS, for instance, more attention from the press than Florsheim; Warby Parker will get featured in roundups of the newest in fashion eyewear right alongside an industry heavyweight like Ray-Ban not because of their size, but because of their innovative generosity.

A nice example from my own career of exceeding expectations came when Focus on the Family, as part of our rebranding under Jim Daly's leadership, created an outreach to Millennials. In one sense, we were doing what the press expected us to do: telling families—in this case younger families, but still—about the ways we could help them navigate their marriages, raise their children and walk out their faith boldly in the public square. That meant, in part, articulating the organization's positions on hot-button cultural issues like abortion and same-sex marriage, which we opposed because we believed the Bible opposes them. That was such an expected thing for us to do, in fact, one could easily argue it was a dog-bites-man story—i.e., a non-story.

But hang on a second. We were sharing these offerings from our value proposition in a way no other group like ours had ever done: via an assistant to the president for Millennial relations, who reported to me as the VP of communications, who was herself a Millennial. Esther Fleece was (and still is) a peerless relationship broker and communicator with a heart for families in crisis that is born of personal tragedy overcome. Her job, as we shorthanded it, was to get others at her age and stage of life to take a second look at Focus if they had been put off by their first encounter—and a first look if they'd never bothered before. We wanted them to see that while we still staunchly believed in the scriptural perspective on marriage and family, we preferred now to engage in more dialogue and less monologue.

The proudly progressive monthly magazine *Mother Jones* saw Esther's hiring as wildly exceeding their expectations. In a major feature headlined "GOP Hipster Makeover?" it wrote:

> (Fleece) notes that Focus' founder, 73-year-old James Dobson, turned the organization into a political force primarily through a radio audience, and 'I haven't listened to much radio lately.' She's helping Focus reach into social media, tweeting about music ('#u2webcast is incredible'), Scripture ('Get the Bible on twitter! New verse every hour') and cars ('looking for SUV suggestions. Safe, good on gas, cute...'.)[42]

A little snarky? Absolutely. *Mother Jones* is, after all, a practitioner of "directed reporting" (see Chapter 2) with an ideological lens diametrically opposed to Focus on the Family's. But we considered the story a hearty man-bites-dog win because it depicted us as an innovator among our peers, and reasonable and respectful while interacting with those with whom we disagreed. It was a high-water mark for Focus 2.0—as we referred to ourselves post-rebranding. I was given the final say in the piece: "Our goal is to recognize what motivates this generation. We need to take what we're already doing"—such as ministering to foster children—"and express it in a way that meets them where they're at."[43]

Exceeding expectations is fun, but nothing compared to the rush of upsetting them. It's biting the dog with platinum teeth—the ultimate exercise in creating news. You not only get the benefits of the resulting story; you get the kudos that come, and stay, when others see you in a different light. You can solidify, change and/or establish a reputation for yourself as an author, expert, speaker, coach and consultant. By exceeding expectations you are delivering a surprise to the news cycle; what the press, and their audiences, thought they'd see is not what they get. You become Steven Seagal's best-known film character, Casey Ryback of *Under Siege* (and its sequel.) Remember? Terrorists take over the Navy battleship on which he is stationed, lock up all the seamen they consider threats, and leave Casey to roam around the galley. He famously claims he's nothing but the below-deck chef—but he surprises his shipmates and the bad guys when he breaks out special-ops skills in thwarting the maniacal plan of a jilted military officer looking to start World War III by swiping the ship's nuclear weapons. Casey upset everyone's expectations, sometimes by building a microwave bomb out of booze and a Brillo Pad, ultimately by gouging out the terrorist mastermind's eye with his thumb and plunging a knife into his skull.

Fear not, upsetting expectations in PR is nowhere near that scientifically illogical or violent. We did it at Focus on the Family

> **Exceeding expectations is fun, but nothing compared to the rush of upsetting them. It's biting the dog with platinum teeth—the ultimate exercise in creating news.**

simply by showing a sense of humor. It was, again, in the midst of our stem-to-stern rebranding effort. We had just "won" an honor in the local progressive newsweekly's reader's poll—as Colorado Springs' No. 1 Claim to Shame. The paper, the *Colorado Springs Independent*, had for years been skeweringly critical of Focus, especially our public-policy advocacy, once even running a photo illustration on its cover of Dr. Dobson with an elephant's trunk, to argue he had sold out to the Republican Party. Our relationship wasn't frosty, it was absolute-zero frozen. So when we got the mass-mailed invitation to the "Best of the Springs" annual gala celebrating the readers' poll winners (which included everything from Best Restaurant to Favorite TV Personality), we were pretty sure they didn't actually expect us to show up. But show up we did.

That's because we weren't just trying to reframe the organization at the national level. We wanted to spotlight our repositioned distinctives in our own backyard, too. To that end, I had hired another impressive Millennial, Rajeev Shaw, as our assistant to the president for community relations. His job was to do with a geographic group (the Front Range of Colorado) what Esther Fleece was doing among her demographic group: get folks to take a fresh look at Focus on the Family. What better place to do that, Rajeev and I reasoned, than at a formal event in which we were being "honored" as a blight on the city's reputation? So we rented tuxedos, had a couple of buttons made that said "We Won the Claim To Shame Award. Ask Us Why We Didn't Deserve It" and partied with our detractors.

The story that resulted from our effort so upset expectations that mere journalism couldn't contain it. It was a literary event, winding up as a story that exemplified Focus under Jim Daly in the book *The Evangelicals You Don't Know: Introducing the Next Generation of Christians*.

Tom Krattenmaker, himself an unabashed progressive, was chatting with Jim about the epithets thrown at him and the ministry through the years by those who oppose it ideologically, and Jim cited

A PRESS RELEASE IMPRESSES LEAST

There was a time, when the PR newswire really was a wire and not a website or email, and reporters wore those stylin' fedoras with a card emblazoned PRESS stuck in the band, that press releases were the coin of the public-relations realm. This is no longer that time.

You will get different counsel from other sources, I'm sure, but I'm convinced the generally most ineffective way to generate coverage for yourself and your offerings is to disseminate a press release. I used to be a reporter, and I rarely even read the press releases that landed on my desk, let alone built a story around one. They are impersonal, imprecise shots across the communications transom—reporters are more likely to feel spammed than impressed. That's why many refer to press releases derisively as a "spray and pray" tactic.

Volume and quality are also working against you. These things are like gnats around the porchlight that is the reporter's inbox. Many are poorly written, full of jargon and lazy superlatives. Yours may be a splendid array of words expertly explaining how you exceed or upset the reporter's expectations, but how slipshod others' work is, combined with that stuffed-up inbox, means your work likely never gets opened.

So what to do? The best avenue for on-ramping your message is more personal contact—a publicist who picks up the phone and has contacts he or she has worked with before, for instance. Sending personalized emails tailored to the beat and background of the reporter you want to attract works, too. If a mass-ish cold-call mailing must be done, make it a news advisory (see Chapter 8)—a more compact piece that clearly explains why a reporter should cover your story and is easily contained on a single page.

his budding friendship with the *Independent*'s publisher, John Weiss, as an example of how he was seeking to change that—one defied expectation at a time.

"Daly is referring to the publisher of the left-leaning *Colorado Springs Independent*, the city's alternative weekly," Krattenmaker writes. "The newspaper has often been sharply critical of Focus, and its readers voted to give the organization the Claim to Shame award in the newspaper's 'Best of 2010' issue. (Maintaining their sense of humor, Schneeberger and

The Fray lead singer, Isaac Slade, acknowledges the crowd after his performance at *A Community Rises*, a 2012 benefit concert for wildfire-ravaged Colorado Springs, Colorado, made possible by the strategic upsetting of press expectations. (Personal photo.)

community relations director Rajeev Shaw attended the awards event and accepted the dubious prize, donning tuxedos for the occasion.) As Daly explains to me, relations took a positive turn."[44] Just how positive is where the story gets not just good, but transformative. Two years of relationship-building later, which saw far fairer coverage of our initiatives and activities in the paper's pages, the city faced a natural catastrophe when a wildfire burned out of control in late June 2012. From a second-floor balcony on the Focus campus, I watched the flames lick their way down the Rocky Mountains to more neighborhoods … and hatched a plan to team up with the *Indy*—we were on a nickname basis now—to stage a benefit concert to raise money for the victims. Together we assembled a team of community leaders and pulled off a July 4th show featuring music from the city's orchestra and Colorado native Isaac Slade, lead singer of the platinum-selling rock band The Fray. We raised about $300,000 for families affected by the blaze.

I was quoted the day after by the Christian magazine *WORLD*, another directed-reporting publication.

"This was not a 'Christian' concert," Schneeberger told me. "No prayer (said), no worship music played. But together, we were able to find that patch of grass we could all stand on to help our city by raising money and modeling community."[45]

'SORRY' SEEMS TO BE THE HARDEST WORD

It's worth a moment's pause to spotlight a specific, and sadly underutilized, way to upset expectations. I learned it from Janet Jackson.

We all remember Janet's "wardrobe malfunction" during the halftime show of Super Bowl XXXVIII in 2004: While finishing up a gyration-rich performance with Justin Timberlake, she and the former boy-bander interacted in such a way that one of her breasts was exposed. Given that football's championship game is not exactly premium cable, but more family fare, the masses went apoplectic, monsooning the NFL, CBS (which aired the game) and the FCC (which fined CBS) with complaints.

Do you remember Janet's response to the furor? She said: "I'm really sorry if I offended anyone."[46]

Read that again. Not "I'm sorry I exposed my northerly goodies to your kids and grandparents." Not "I'm sorry the stunt Justin and I planned was in poor taste." Not even just "I'm sorry." She said she was sorry *if* anyone was offended.

And that's the lesson Janet Jackson taught me that I've passed along since to anybody who'll listen. Apologies aren't sincere if they contain the word "if." And you will earn major PR points if you don't compound a screw-up with a Janet Jackson Apology.

Think about it. When was the last time you heard someone the media has cause to chase around with a microphone offer a no-ifs-ands-or-buts "I'm sorry"? It's exceedingly rare, because as a society we've come to view admitting a mistake as weakness. It is anything but. Not only does it take fortitude of character to acknowledge a wrong, it will resonate with your audience precisely because it is so rare. You will earn points, not lose them, for having the guts and integrity to raise your hand and take the foul.

Quickly, here's the anatomy of a good apology in public (or private, for that matter) relations: 1) as already discussed, no ifs, ands or buts—own it; 2) be specific about what you're sorry for, and indicate you know what you did was irresponsible or immature or dangerous or whatever makes it something you have to apologize for; and 3) go the extra mile and ask for forgiveness. Bundle those together and you'll also be better insulated from shouts of "You're only sorry you got caught" or criticism that you're just rotely saying the words to get yourself off the hook.

Thanks for the wisdom, Janet. Or Miss Jackson, if you're nasty.

> **Not only does it take fortitude of character to acknowledge a wrong, it will resonate with your audience precisely because it is so rare. You will earn points, not lose them, for having the guts and integrity to raise your hand and take the foul.**

A WORD ABOUT PRESIDENT TRUMP

Can I be honest? I've been putting off writing this section of the book. But now that I'm finishing up the chapter on effective PR strategy, I can't justify avoiding it any longer. I mean, how do you cover this topic without mentioning the 45th president of the United States, who makes a lot of news but follows none of the strategic suggestions I've laid out here? Sure, it's the third rail of non-political discourse: Say something perceived as either supportive or critical of Donald Trump and you risk losing friends, clients, even family. So it's best in some cases to not mention him at all. And yet ... somebody reading these words right now—maybe it's you—is processing all the things I've been recommending and thinking, "Why don't any of these stratagems apply to Donald Trump? And if he doesn't have to do them, why do I?"

The answer to the first question is, "I don't know." The answer to the second is, "Because you're not Donald Trump." Donald Trump is a PR savant. That does not mean I think he is a PR genius; only that I think the rules that govern the communications universe the rest of us have to live in do not occupy his atmosphere. He can yell at and Tweet-bomb his media detractors—calling them "losers" and worse, calling their publications and shows "failures" and worse—and not lose supporters. In fact, rants of that nature tend to invigorate those who back him. He can make outsized claims about his accomplishments, get caught saying terrible things on a hot mic, and not alienate those same supporters.

All of this has led me to a conclusion that is purely professional, not political. I say it not as a criticism of President Trump, but as an admonishment to you not to follow in his newsmaking footsteps. That is because what works for him will not work for you. You need to master and apply public relations. And Donald Trump doesn't practice public relations. He practices public retaliations.

President Trump operates from the premise that his base—be they fans of *The Apprentice* or voters who punched the chad next to his name—doesn't like or trust the "mainstream media." So he has zero qualms about doing any of those things described above while interacting with them. And those who oppose him? They are already aghast at everything he says and does. What exactly is the effect of them becoming aghast-er? Will his Teflon coating be scratched because they now Really, Really, Really Super Big-Time No, Honest, We So Couldn't Oppose Him More?

Nope.

Donald Trump knows, I'd argue better than anyone, how to maneuver the political and ideological wedge that exists in American culture. George Bush famously called himself a "uniter, not a divider." Donald Trump gleefully acts as the exact opposite, Bizarro Bush in Superman terms, when getting his message out—whether via a 3 a.m., post-*SNL* Twitter strafing or a press conference. It works for him, at least in the way he wants it to. It will not work for you in the same way. So don't try it. Please.

Whew. I got through it. Hopefully you don't want to beat me up now like Steven Seagal with a cue ball wrapped in a bar towel.

NEXT UP

I made reference, in the section immediately prior, to this chapter being about PR strategy. While I haven't come right out and said it until now, each chapter has focused on a single step in the process of—you thought I forgot, didn't you?—wisely leveraging expectations and opportunities through strategically crafted and applied public relations. Chapter 1 was all about the *importance* of the art. Chapter 2, the *environment* of the mediasphere. Chapter 3, the *identity* you bring to your newsmaking efforts. Chapter 4, the *opportunities* available to you to have your message heard. And now that we've covered *strategy*, let's move on to *achievement*, or how to keep news stories coming once the proper foundations have been laid and tested. You ready?

6

Commit News

Have you ever caught a commercial for your local TV newscast when, all of a sudden, right there with your hometown anchor(s), appears the guy (or gal) who sits behind the desk for the national evening news— be it Jeff Glor (CBS), Lester Holt (NBC) or David Muir (ABC)? These promotional spots are usually filmed over a long day at a network's annual affiliate gathering. They involve a rapid-fire cattle call of sorts: Local newsies are paraded before the national star, they trade essentially the same scripted banter whether it's Poughkeepsie or Portsmouth and move along as quickly as they came in. By the end of the day, upwards of 100 local stations go home with an ad that makes it appear their newsreaders are buddy-buddy with the big dogs.

A similar ritual occurs in nationally syndicated radio. The host with six- or seven-digit audience numbers records or drops in live for a few minutes with a local affiliate that airs his or her program. They trade happy talk with one of the homegrown hosts for a couple of minutes. The idea is the same as in TV—to add gravitas to the talker with the smaller audience by spotlighting him or her interacting with the individual with the bigger one. During my time at Focus on the Family under the leadership of Dr. James Dobson, when his daily radio show reached more than 7 million listeners in the US on hundreds of radio stations in all 50 states, ringing up local hosts was a couple-of-times-a-week calendar item for Dr. Dobson.

So, when he was scheduled to call into a Dallas affiliate on January 13, 2008, my PR Spidey-sense didn't tingle in the slightest. This wasn't an interview; it was a promo. A couple of minutes of mutual admiration society between him and the local host talking about how much the host loved Focus and how much Focus appreciated being broadcast on the Dallas affiliate … and we'd be on to the next to-do list item. Except nobody told the host any of this.

Instead of just swapping some gee-you're-swells with Dr. Dobson, the host used the opportunity to ask him some questions about the pending presidential election, which was witnessing the rise of candidate John McCain as the front-runner for the GOP nomination. Dr. Dobson was, at the time, the highest-profile and most politically influential Christian leader in the country, so bully for the host in seizing the moment. Dr. Dobson, when asked about a McCain candidacy, listed a few of the Arizona senator's policy positions that troubled him, said he could never vote for him and ended the conversation squarely in Sound-Bite City: "I pray that we don't get stuck with him."

And just like that, it was time to make the PR donuts.

The news firestorm that followed was something out of an Irwin Allen movie. The host posted the conversation, which now had become an "interview" rather than a "promotion." *World Net Daily*, a website perhaps best described as the Christian version of *The Drudge Report*, reported on Dr. Dobson's comments. Then the mainstream media (see the PR-Verb in Chapter 3 to refresh your memory as to why you should scold me for that) picked up the story in items by CNN, *Politico* and The Associated Press. Then *The Drudge Report* itself linked to the coverage. The next day, less than 24 hours after Dr. Dobson uttered the words, Sen. McCain was asked about them as he stepped off his campaign bus at the day's first whistle-stop. The circle was complete: Dr. Dobson had started out doing a broadcast grip-and-grin and wound up committing news.[47]

I recount this story for two reasons: 1) To ensure you grasp the reality that you can, as an author, expert, speaker, coach and/or consultant, create news. The subtitle of this book, the part about making news that matters, is not just a (hopefully) clever turn of phrase. It is 100-proof truth. You are a messaging magician, able to conjure up news where none exists. You don't have to wait for it, hope for it, worry about missing out on it. You can *make* it. And you should. In fact, you must if you want to achieve your goal of broadening your impact and influence. When you do, though, you must be strategic and intentional about it. That's reason-for-this-story No. 2) Making news should always be a conscious undertaking. As I've mentioned till *you're* probably blue in the face, PR is the—let me hear you in the cheap seats!—wise leveraging of opportunities and expectations of the media and the masses. You can't leverage either by happenstance, any more than Steven Seagal can stumble his way into leveraging the momentum of a guy bum-rushing him to gain the upper fist.

Committing news needs to be as focused a part of your business plan/daily routine as making whatever widgets you manufacture—be they products or services—under your brand.

Conscious leveraging was sorely lacking in the Dr. Dobson/Sen. McCain incident—news just sort of happened when a conversation turned into an interview, and a personal opinion expressed in less-than-ideal language for a Christian leader—"I pray we don't get stuck with him"—made the entire proceeding all the juicier. News was definitely committed, but not wisely or thoughtfully so. And Dr. Dobson's reputation took a ding because of it—especially when, months later, he recanted his pledge not to cast a ballot for McCain. He changed his mind after the nominee selected as his running mate then-Alaska Gov. Sarah Palin, who shared Dr. Dobson's positions on the social issues that most informed his vote.

Committing news, at least the kind you want to commit, requires, well, commitment. It needs to be as focused a part of your business plan/daily routine as making whatever widgets you manufacture—be they products or services—under your brand. Think of it as using the combined strength of both of your arms to carry something heavy and/or bulky. The heavy object is your desire to make news that matters. One arm is the "strategically crafted" part of PR—the infrastructure and awareness that allow you to leverage opportunities and expectations. The other arm is the "applied" part: doing something with vision and verve that flows naturally from your brand promise and value proposition and which is—and here's where we missed the mark in the McCain example—an intentional act done to make news that will, by its nature, also matter.

'WE'RE TAKING ON WATER!'

No one could argue that Paramount Pictures went with the conventional choice when it turned over its 2014 big-screen adaptation of the biblical story of Noah to director Darren Aronofsky. The indie auteur behind such dark classics as *Black Swan* and *The Wrestler* had not shown a single Cecil B. DeMille inclination in his career up to the point he was given keys to the ark by the studio—and it showed in the finished product. This was not the cute kids Sunday school story of animals marching two-by-two aboard the boat past a smiling old man with a long white beard. It was a psychological action drama starring Russell Crowe as the brooding title character and featuring everything from giant walking-and-talking rock creatures to an evil and sadistic stowaway on the perilous journey through the flood. And then there was the little matter of—spoiler alert!—Noah deciding God called him not to save mankind but to wipe its sinful stain from the earth, a task he pursues with such single-minded passion he attempts to stab his twin granddaughters to death. Oh, yeah, and Aronofsky had declared himself an atheist in an interview a few years earlier, confessing that "I'm Godless. I've had to make my God, and my God is narrative filmmaking."[48]

How in the world—Old Testament or New—do you market that movie to audiences who believe in God and revere the Scriptures? Especially in what the press had come to call "The Year of the Bible" in Hollywood? Thanks to the record-breaking success of the Roma Downey/Mark Burnett miniseries *The Bible* in 2013, 2014 was unfurling a holy scroll's worth of religiously themed fare. There was *Son of God*, Downey and Burnett's big-screen adaptation of the Jesus bits of *The Bible*, plus *Heaven is for Real, God's Not Dead* and *Exodus: Gods and Kings* also hitting theaters in the span of several months. Well, I can tell you how you market *Noah* to faith audiences in that environment because I did it—as head of publicity for Grace Hill Media, the boutique PR firm that launched the outreach-to-the-churched movement in Tinseltown after the titanic success of Mel Gibson's *The Passion of the Christ* in 2004. What did my colleagues and I do? We committed news—specifically news in the faith-based press that would reach faith-based listeners, viewers and readers.

The backlash against the film, before it was even finished, based on Aronofsky's pedigree and a review of an early draft of a script published online, was truly a tidal wave of biblical-plague proportions. Typical of the froth was this from Christian screenwriter Brian Godawa: "This movie will be rejected by millions of devoted Bible readers worldwide because once again it subverts their own sacred narrative with a political agenda of pagan earth religion that is offensive to their Faith. In a very real sense it engages in the very sin of the primeval history in Genesis: A denial of the image of God in man."[50] The headline of his essay, in case readers didn't want to wade too far in to get to his point, was "Darren Aronofsky's Noah: Environmentalist Wacko."

Committing news in the midst of this mess meant creating the one thing that did not exist in all the tongue-wagging over the movie: Christians who had actually seen it. We figured many reasonable men and women of faith would discern that *Noah*, for all its director's viewpoints that were not rooted in Scripture, was faithful to the biblical story in the way that mattered most: capturing the character of God (not his film character; because He doesn't appear and is, in fact, only

FACTS ARE STUBBORNLY USEFUL THINGS

You know how I feel about spin, the word and the practice, if you've read Chapter 3. It makes PR out to be more about style than substance, to the point of implying we'd shade or shuck the truth in order to make a point that helps us make news. Yes, it's true—as I also said in Chapter 3—that a strategic framing of the issues you're talking about can go a long way to persuading an audience to your point of view. But nothing has been invented in the communication arts to date to beat marshaling good old-fashioned facts that prove your point.

You want to commit news? Commit to presenting to the press the most compelling facts you can in support of your efforts.

Exhibit A: A story I was quoted in on the eve of the 2016 fall TV season's premiere. Controversy was being ginned up at the alleged racial bias of CBS for featuring only white males in lead roles in its slate of new programming. I thought I blew a hole in that contention pretty shrewdly and succinctly by relying on nothing more elaborate than an indisputable fact.

"It's ironic CBS is being singled out as racially insensitive," I told the online publication *Popzette*, "when, just last season, in *Supergirl*, producers re-imagined Jimmy Olsen from the goofy white kid photographer in the comics and all previous films and TV shows, into a serious, sexy, African-American head of the newspaper art department."[49]

Expectations upset. News committed. Good day at the PR office.

referenced as The Creator. But His spiritual character.) When those men and women of faith then discussed their reaction to the film, we concluded, we would be upsetting expectations.

We were honest and transparent that there was, indeed, a lot of stuff in the movie that isn't in the Bible. We framed that as narrative necessity, pointing out that Scripture, for instance, never names Noah's wife and that the man himself doesn't even speak until the end of the story ("Starring Russell Crowe in his first silent-movie performance!".) We reminded every person we showed the film to in advance that the typical *Saturday Night Live* skit had more material on which to base a motion picture than the Genesis account of Noah and the ark. We pointed out that some of the loudest voices bemoaning the film's "biblical inaccuracy" often tried to answer questions like, "What was Noah's reaction when God called him to build the ark?"—despite Scripture offering no record of his response. We made sure these Christian advance viewers understood they were seeing an action film, not reading the NDAV Bible—the New Darren Aronofsky Version.

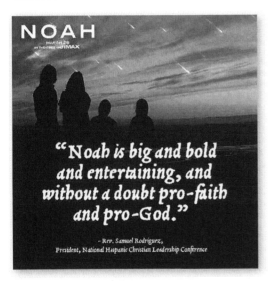

More than a dozen Christian leaders of varying denominations and demographics offered hearty endorsements of *Noah*, counteracting the speculation in church circles that the big-budget film gave God and the Bible a black eye. (NCHLC[51])

The goal of all this was simple: We wanted to wrest control back from those voices who were telling people of faith they would be dishonoring God by seeing the movie. We didn't tell them they had to like it, only that they wouldn't be guilty of heresy if they saw it.

The results were exactly what we hoped for, allowing us to create marketing materials spotlighting some of the most influential faith leaders in the country using these words to describe the film: "brilliant," "bold," "spectacular," "pro-God," "amazing," "powerful," "artistic," "profound," "riveting," "astonishing," "path-breaking," "deeply important," "beautiful," "visually stunning" and "a rare gift." Again, these were reactions that upset the expectations in the culture that Christians would want to burn the movie at the stake. Even better from a purely PR perspective, though, our efforts did indeed make news, including a piece from filmmaker and blogger Phil Cooke in which he laid out eight reasons why he recommended his fellow Christians see the film. No. 6 was exactly the kind of buzz we wanted to create. He wrote:

> Whatever extra-Biblical elements there are in the film, that doesn't overcome the fact that Paramount Studios is spending hundreds of millions of dollars to produce and promote a Bible story. This will be a national conversation that millions will participate in, and *Noah* will be water cooler conversation for the next 6 months. What an opportunity for the Christian community! Instead of condemning it outright, let's join the conversation. Rarely does an event come along that begs us to present our side of the story. But if we don't see the movie, we'll be wasting the opportunity.[52]

Noah went on to earn a robust $43.7 million at the box office its opening weekend, finishing in the top spot, and wound up grossing more than $101 million in the US during its theatrical run. What's more, the very thing Cooke predicted (and the very opposite of what Godawa predicted) happened. In the days after *Noah* premiered in theaters on March 28, 2014, the website *BibleGateway.com* reported a 223 percent increase from the previous weekend in the number of people who looked up the Noah story in Genesis chapters 6 through 9.[53] Even more remarkable, *YouVersion*, the No. 1 Bible smartphone app, saw a 300 percent increase in users opening the biblical account of Noah in the US—and a 245 percent increase globally.[54] During a time when the weekend movie buzz was about a Harry Potter book when it wasn't about a comic book, America was talking about the Good Book.

Those were impressive results by Hollywood and Bible-believer standards, to be sure. But how did they score on the committing news scale? Returning to my two-arms-lifting-something-heavy-and-bulky analogy, we had the strategic arm covered: We upset the expectations of an audience that had heard a string of bad things about the movie for its supposed blasphemous content. We also had the applied arm covered, by acting to change the cultural discussion. We flipped the script, to be overly clever about it, by showing open-minded Christians the movie in advance and sharing their positive reactions with a wider swath of people inside and outside the church. In the end, we made the case that the God Christians believe in and the god Darren Aronofsky believes in—narrative filmmaking—could march two-by-two like oxen onto the ark. And we've got the committed news—man-bites-dog style—to prove it.

STRANGE, NEWSWORTHY BEDFELLOWS

At this point you may be thinking, "I'm not a major movie studio with hundreds of millions to spend on PR. I don't have the star power of Russell Crowe to draw attention to my brand, products and services. What in the heck were those giant walking-and-talking rock creatures a few paragraphs ago?" I have no answer for the last question, because, well, there is no reasonable explanation for them. Paging Mr. Aronofsky! But I can help you with the first two observations—and you'll like what you hear. News is no respecter of blockbuster budgets or Academy Awards; it will allow itself to be committed on a shoestring and to any size audience you choose. By way of illustration, let's revisit Focus on the Family's relationship with the local progressive newsweekly the *Independent*—first discussed last chapter. To briefly recap: They didn't like us. We

> **News is no respecter of blockbuster budgets or Academy Awards; it will allow itself to be committed on a shoestring and to any size audience you choose.**

upset their expectations. We started working together where our ideals overlapped for the good of our shared community.

While the benefit concert to aid wildfire victims on Independence Day 2012 was the high-water mark of our collaboration during my days at Focus, our first partnership was also rewarding—and took the entire city of Colorado Springs by surprise. It was such a prodigious bite to the news dog that, in announcing it to the press, we didn't even have to tell them what we were doing to get their attention. Every TV station in town and the daily newspaper showed up to cover our joint news conference simply because it was a joint news conference. All we said in our news advisory was that Focus on the Family and the *Independent* were undertaking a shared community initiative. It could have been an old-school fundraising car wash or a kids' front-yard lemonade stand and it still would have committed news.

It was something much more meaningful, though. Focus had recently launched an outreach called Wait No More (run by my dear friend Kelly Rosati, who so graciously wrote the foreword to this book), an ambitious effort to persuade families nationwide to adopt children out of foster-care. The program was born out of a painful past and simple math: Jim Daly, our president, was himself an orphan. He had been abandoned by his alcoholic father at age 5, then lost his mother to cancer four years later—a wound deepened when his stepfather also abandoned Jim, the youngest of five children, and his siblings to fend for themselves hours after their mother's funeral. Jim spent time in the foster-care system, which today has more than 100,000 children in it. Compare that number to the 300,000 churches nationwide, and you can see the simple math behind the thrust of Wait No More: to wipe clean the foster-care rolls in the US.[55]

The *Independent* had no formal foster-care initiatives, but was involved in promoting and serving several charities in Colorado Springs. Publisher John Weiss believed foster families were too-often-unsung heroes, and had long looked for an opportunity to put his megaphone behind an effort to honor and assist those who stepped

True confession: I was near tears an hour before this news conference announcing the first collaboration between Focus on the Family and the *Independent*, when I caught a glimpse of the organizations' banners hanging in unison. *Indy* Publisher John Weiss (left) and Focus President Jim Daly committed man-bites-dog news that day—and remain friends and frequent partners on community projects today. (Personal photo.)

forward to care for the kids who desperately needed the stability they provided. And thus was born A Fostering Celebration, the event our groups co-sponsored, which served the goals of both organizations. It gave foster families a pat on the back and a helping hand (their top priority), while encouraging the community at large to remove the adjective from as many foster children as possible (our top priority.) The union not only led to a successful event that served about 50 families in the region but also committed news that advanced the brand and mission of both organizations.

"They don't always see eye-to-eye, but now Focus on the Family and the *Colorado Springs Independent* are teaming up to help support foster care families in the Pikes Peak area," began a report from the local CBS affiliate, KKTV.

The announcement was made Monday during a news conference held with Jim Daly, Focus on the Family President, and John Weiss, publisher of the *Independent*.

'When I heard what they were doing with foster care, which is trying to support the families which are adopting the kids, giving them everything from a night out without the kids, to cleaning to cooking … we thought this was wonderful,' said Weiss.

For Jim Daly the focus on the foster care community is personal. … 'I was in foster care for a year, and it was not a tremendously positive experience for me.' Daly added, 'I was one of these kids, so I know firsthand how important a stable, loving home environment is to them.'[56]

It's important to remember that although Focus on the Family has a global footprint, with a commensurate budget, we were operating regionally at most in this instance. We wanted to make news that made a difference in our own backyard—and trust me when I tell you, as the guy who managed the budget for community relations, we were not talking Hollywood-marketing-type money. Not even a sliver of that. So the resulting coverage wasn't financed or featured as anything other than a local news story. And that was just fine with us.

XLIV-CALIBER SUCCESS

If you're fortunate as an author, expert, speaker, coach and/or consultant, as you consistently apply the lessons of this book, you will, at least once in your public life, not just commit news, but commit news with a contrail. You will make news that matters *and* leaves a mark. The masses won't just become aware of you and your products and services; they will remember you and your products and services. You'll stop making headlines with the story eventually, but that's OK. Because you will have made history.

That's what we did at Focus on the Family in late January/early February 2010. Over an exhausting and exhilarating three weeks, we galvanized the attention of the nation (and even some other parts of the world) on one of the foundational pillars of our organization. We did it with a combination of advertising and public relations—and I bet you can guess by now which one accounted for most of the buzz. To have the value of the earned media outpace the value of the paid media by a factor of 10 was a pretty tall order, too, when the ad in question wasn't printed in the weekly *Pennysaver*. It was broadcast during Super Bowl XLIV—and became the most talked-about big-game commercial in a generation.

A lot of things had to go right, and we had to do a lot of things right, to commit news on such a gargantuan scale. Sure, we had a head start by buying space during the most watched television event of the year. And our spot featured quarterback Tim Tebow, fresh out of college after winning the Heisman Trophy and two national championships at the University of Florida. His celebrity didn't hurt. Tebow also wore his Christianity on his sleeve—and in his eye black, where he printed Bible verses for each game, sending hundreds of thousands of fans watching at home scurrying to Google during commercial breaks to look up what James 1:2–4 or Mark 8:36 said. So he was a bit of a media lightning rod to boot. The ad would be Tebow's first post-collegiate endorsement deal—and it wasn't with Nike or Gatorade, but with a family help organization that was beloved by its hundreds of thousands of constituents yet was hardly a household name in terms of how many households watched the NFL's championship game. That added another leveragable asset to our newsmaking arsenal, upsetting the expectations of a culture accustomed to athletes loosed from the confines of amateur eligibility rules grabbing the biggest wad of cash thrust in their direction.

In the end, though, none of that fueled our drive to more than $30 million in AVE—earned media—by the time the Indianapolis Colts kicked off to the New Orleans Saints at Miami's Sun Life Stadium on

February 7. That high-octane achievement came courtesy of the content of the ad itself, which was exactly what was expected of Focus on the Family in subject matter, but nothing at all what was expected of us in execution. When we told our neighbor newspaper, *The Denver Post*, on January 15 that we were running a Super Bowl ad, we said only that it featured Tim and his Mom, Pam, who "share our respect for life and our passion for helping families thrive."[57] The paucity of information was intentional. We knew others would fill in the blanks about what story the ad might tell, because Pam had been telling one that spotlighted the Tebow family's "respect for life" for years on the public-speaking circuit. It was easily discoverable with a couple of keystrokes and a web browser.

Pam Tebow is a sweet-spoken woman whose elegant bearing belies her hardscrabble history of serving with her husband as a missionary in impoverished regions of the world. While pregnant with Tim in the Philippines on one such missions trip, she developed medical complications and was urged by local doctors to terminate her pregnancy. Because of her pro-life convictions and faith, she ignored the doctors' advice, prayed for the health and safety of her unborn child and carried Tim to term. It was a compelling story no matter who her baby grew up to be. That he grew up to be arguably the greatest college football player of all time gave it a little extra narrative oomph. For Focus on the Family, since its inception in 1977 an unabashed champion of the lives of children in the womb, it was exactly the kind of story everybody figured we'd tell. But they miscalculated how we'd tell it—at least our most vocal critics did. And that, to borrow from the X's and O's of football and the start of Chapter 3, was precisely the opening we needed to score touchdown after touchdown after ... you get the idea.

Groups at ideological odds with us on life issues did more than just cry havoc to the media. They used a word that intoxicates journalists like catnip intoxicates tabbies: boycott. The Women's Media Center led the litter, demanding CBS refuse to air the ad or else, threatening

A behind-the-scenes shot from the green room during filming of
the Focus on the Family Super Bowl commercial featuring
Tim Tebow. (Personal photo.)

advertisers with tune-outs if their terms were not met. The Super
Bowl, they maintained, was no place for sharp-edged political debates
over abortion rights —which they assumed our commercial was even
though they hadn't seen it. No one had, except us, and what they were
caterwauling about was not what we had scripted and filmed. Remember
our discussion in Chapter 3 about our year-long effort to rebrand the
organization as less about monologue and more about dialogue?
Those stories earlier in this chapter and in Chapter 4 about reaching
out to and working with groups who disagreed with us? Apparently
the Women's Media Center and other left-leaning individuals and
organizations weren't paying attention to the changes forged by Focus
2.0, because the ad they imagined we produced sounded a lot like the
worst stereotype they could dream up of something manufactured by
Focus Classic, Culture Wars Edition.

That's the expectation we leveraged with Herculean heft. Our
goal was to start a respectful national dialogue about how choosing
life in an unplanned pregnancy was every bit as rational a choice as
terminating it. And the 30-second spot was the perfect tool for doing

that. It begins with a smiling Pam, alone, looking at a picture of and talking about her "miracle baby." She explains how he "almost didn't make it into this world." Recalls how hard it was to have nearly "lost him" many times. Then she smiles, the music grows more upbeat, and she says "he's all grown up now." She still worries about his health, she confesses, because "with all our family's been through, we've had to be tough." That's the cue for Tim (or a special effect of him) to rush in from stage right to "tackle" Pam (or her CGI doppelganger.) We hear an "oof." The smiling mother and son hop to their feet. Pam playfully scolds him for interrupting their family story. Tim asks, "Do you still worry about me, Mom?" "Well, yeah," she replies. "You're not nearly as tough as I am." And … scene.

And what a scene it turned into.

A signed memento from Focus on the Family's Tim Tebow Super Bowl commercial highlights the stats of the effort. (Personal photo.)

That $30-million-plus in earned media came from stories in or on, in part, and in alphabetical order: *ABC World News Tonight, Advertising Age, Adweek, America Live with Megyn Kelly* (when she was still with Fox News), *Around the Horn* (ESPN), The Associated Press, *The Atlantic, The Boston Globe, CBS Evening News, Chicago Tribune, Christianity Today, CNN This Morning, The Dallas Morning News,* ESPN News, *Forbes, The Fox Report with Shepard Smith, Good Morning America, Hannity,* Headline News, *Huffington Post, Human Events, Jimmy Kimmel Live, Larry King Live, Los Angeles Times,* MTV, *New Republic, New York Daily News, The New Yorker, The New York Times, Nightline, The Philadelphia Inquirer, Rachel Maddow,* Reuters, *Rush Limbaugh, San Francisco Chronicle, Saturday Night Live, Sports Center, The View, Time,* TMZ, *Today,* USA *Today,* VH1, *The Washington Post* and Yahoo! News. The BBC and plenty of Canadian outlets got in on the act, as well. Even Al Jazeera tried — but we declined their offer. Adding together the circulations of the publications and ratings of the broadcasts of every news story generated by the ad, the total number of impressions created — i.e., the number of people who had the opportunity to see or hear about it — was more than 7 billion. Camp on that number for a second. That's more than the total number of people alive in the world at the time, which means millions of people were "impressed" more than once.

But the impact of the ad went far beyond the sheer number of stories. Where it truly allowed us to commit news was in the nature of the stories. Our voice was not the strident, disapproving one — as it had been, if I'm being brutally honest, so many times in the past. We were the group that simply wanted to "celebrate family and celebrate life" — as I said personally in interviews scores of times and we were quoted organizationally as saying hundreds of times. As appearance after appearance unfurled, and CBS steadfastly refused to pull the ad, we started to see advocacy organizations and news outlets that could not have disagreed with us more on sanctity-of-life issues coming to our defense, decrying the opposition we were getting as an attempt to stifle our free speech. Two of the pieces that laid the largest bite into the dog: a *Washington Post* op-ed by the head of NARAL Pro-Choice America, the No. 1 abortion-rights lobbyist group in the country, saying their movement could learn a thing or two from ours[58]; and a *New York Times* editorial—an institutional statement by the Gray Lady herself—that stiff-armed the efforts of those trying to block our ad as "puzzling" and "dismaying."[59]

We could not, of course, claim full credit for making the story of our Super Bowl commercial the blot-out-the-sun, full-on viral news event it turned out to be. Much of that momentum came from the controversy ginned up by the protesters. Yes, we slicked our figurative hair back and tied it in an imaginary ponytail, leveraging that momentum to our advantage in best Steven Seagal style. But there were other key things we did right that speak to the essence of committing news. For starters, we took a risk. We were a nonprofit organization in a tough economy that raised $3 million independent of our operating budget to create an opportunity to tell the largest TV audience of the year about the distinctives of our value proposition. The ad ended with an invitation to see Pam Tebow's full story at our website—and the video of that story was viewed more than 1.5 million times. Those who visited also learned about the myriad other programs we offered to help families in crisis … or just in need of encouragement. You probably don't have $3 million lying about. I'm guessing it may not be a cakewalk for you to raise that amount. But you do have something to offer to the audiences you reach via the news coverage that features you. What's the most audacious thing you can do, the most calculated risk you can take to draw attention to it? It doesn't have to cost a cent.

Another thing we did right—and whenever you set out to commit news you need to do the same—is that we had a plan and the discipline not to deviate from it, despite some twists and turns worthy of an M. Night Shyamalan movie, at least one of the early ones that were good. We decided from the jump that we would not show the commercial before it aired—something that already had become a popular tactic for Super Bowl advertisers given the attention paid to the spots in

> **Another thing we did right— and whenever you set out to commit news you need to do the same—is that we had a plan and the discipline not to deviate from it.**

the weeks leading up to the game. Even more, we committed to not revealing the ad's content, or even confirming it was a "pro-life" spot, despite the runaway speculation. Our refusal to budge on leaking the ad early cost us an appearance on *The O'Reilly Factor*—then cable news' No. 1 talk show. That was a price we were willing to pay, because to reveal the ad early would have killed the story deader than Gino Felino killed Richie Madano. We knew that the surprise of what the ad really was—a sweet depiction of a mother and son who deeply, demonstrably loved one another, as I said over and over and over again in interviews—would be what stuck in people's minds after this was all over. We wanted to ensure our detractors had more time to speculate that we planned a divisive, even graphic political anti-abortion screed. That would allow us, when the ad finally did air, to make the boldest big-stage declaration possible that this was not your father's Focus on the Family.

At the beginning of this chapter I said the subtitle of this book is not just a (hopefully) clever turn of phrase, but 100-proof truth. Two final results of Focus on the Family's Super Bowl ad experience bear that out. They are both rooted in the commercial's, and the organization's, pro-life missions. I mention them here not to make a political or ideological point, but to offer evidence of how making news can, indeed, make a difference that aligns with the goals and values of those who make it.

Result No. 1 comes from research conducted by The Barna Group after the spot aired. It found that 6 percent of those who saw the ad said it caused them to "personally reconsider their opinion about abortion." At first blush, that doesn't sound terribly impressive. But consider that

106.5 million people tuned into the game—making it, at the time, the most watched TV program in history.[60] According to Barna's polling, 43 percent of those who watched the game said they saw the Tebow ad. That's 45.7 million people.[61] And 6 percent of 45.7 million? 2,742,000. That's how many people who saw a pro-life ad from a pro-life group said it caused them to "personally reconsider their opinion about abortion."[62] Does that mean they changed their opinion to one aligned with Focus' view? No. It doesn't mean they changed their opinion at all. But it does mean the ad made them *think* about an issue central to Focus' *raison d'etre*. I can tell you, because I was in the office, seeing those poll results made for a good day at the office.

But not as good as the day we got the letter behind Result No. 2. It was from a young woman named Susan Wood, who said … hang on. I'll let Susan tell you herself. A full transcript of her letter no longer exists online, but I still have a copy:

> "I need to thank you so much. It's not like me to reach out to strangers or agencies for help. I was truly feeling lost. I saw the ad during the Super Bowl and it stuck in my head. I feel like that commercial was made to reach out to me.
>
> "Later that week I googled it and watched the ad over and over. Then I went to your website and watched the related interview. I felt drawn to reach out to you and I am so glad that I did. You may think that all you did was email me back, but you did so much more than that!!! You gave me hope and encouragement. You let me know that if I need help it's out there. (I went to the related website you suggested in your email.) You reminded me that I can't be perfect, but God loves me.
>
> "You also gave me a wake up call. Why was I worrying about what the baby's father wanted me to do? I am always trying to make other people happy. I kept thinking that unless I have an abortion, he won't be happy. Well, you put the focus back where it belongs. It doesn't matter what makes him happy, or me happy for that matter. It's about what will make God happy. I tried to convince the father

of this and he wouldn't listen. I just kept telling myself what you said about how I can't control how others feel about my pregnancy.

"Once I made the decision that it didn't matter what he says or thinks, I'm keeping the baby, I felt so much better! I am excited. I do want to be a mom and I will do my best (although we know I'll be far from perfect) for this baby. I mean I'm scared, too. I have a lot to figure out, especially financially, but I will put my trust in God.

The author with baby Avita Grace, Susan Wood's daughter whose life was saved by Focus on the Family's Super Bowl commercial. "Avita," loosely translated from Spanish, means "life." (Personal photo.)

"I think I was partly afraid that God was mad at me for getting pregnant out of wedlock. While I know he isn't proud of me for it, thank you for reminding me that he still loves me. I didn't need to compound one sin with another. My mistake can't be erased, but I can ask for forgiveness. The father is mad at me and says I'm ruining his life. That's ok. I can not control him or his feelings. I can only protect the baby.

"I can not thank you enough for putting me back on the right track and reminding me what actually matters in life. I don't know how I forgot something so important, but I did. Your organization, through the Super Bowl ad and your thoughtful email, saved this baby's life. I have no doubt about that. And in the process maybe you saved my soul.

"Words just can not express my gratitude, but thank you, thank you, thank you!"

Rubber has never met more meaningful road for me when it comes to committing news. It's a feeling that is eminently available to you, too. It all boils down to whether the story your efforts create successfully advances your goals and agenda—whatever they might be. In this example, just as in the earlier explorations of Focus' partnership with the *Independent* and Grace Hill Media's marketing of *Noah*, the answer is a resounding "yes."

NEXT UP

Nobody's perfect—in PR or anything else. The inescapable truth of taking your message to the masses via the mediasphere is that there will be times you wish you hadn't. There is such a thing as bad press, and sometimes you'll be the one whose mistake causes it. Sometimes external factors will conspire to create a crisis you need to dig yourself out of. Those will not be good days. But they are survivable days. How do you prepare for those rough patches, ride them out, even flip them into assets? Let's find out.

7

$#!+ is Survivable

I've mentioned a few times that my career, at least at the time of this writing, is pretty much evenly split between journalism and PR. I spent the first 15 years as a reporter and editor at small to midsized newspapers (and one major one), and the last 15 doing public-relations work. They are, I've pointed out, two sides of the same denominational coin—even if one has Susan B. Anthony's image etched into it and one has Sacagawea's. Both disciplines require chasing the story—the journalist to report news, the PR pro to make it. Both pursuits are most fulfilling when the story you catch involves a man biting a dog, instead of a dog biting a man. And both, when practiced long enough, will bring the practitioner into contact with mistake and crisis. Yep, no matter which side of the microphone you're on, scenarios that cause somebody to swear will sneak up and surprise you. The good news is, they don't have to bury you.

That said, both mistakes and crises are, alas, generally easier for journalists to weather than for public-relations types and their clients. A news outlet messes something up, and it publishes or issues a correction. Even if that correction requires the dismissal of the reporter who made the mistake, for, in the worst-case scenario, doing so maliciously, the news outlet will live to report another day. Credibility may be dinged for a while, but the 24-hour news cycle breeds short memories. The individual journalist, if he or she didn't outright lie but just misreported, will likely also survive with career intact. Something more insidious than being wrong, as a rule, needs to occur for there to be lasting damage. Once in my reporting days, for instance, I wrote a news item about Students Against Drunk Driving (SADD), and meant to call it a "peer-driven" group. Except I called it a "beer-driven" group. Later, during my days as an editorial page editor, I quoted a community leader describing his experience in "public life." Except I typed "pubic life." The worst one was when I wrote a Page 1 piece about someone charged with a terrible crime, the details of which have been lost to history as it lives on in my brain. What has remained, though, is my recollection that I mixed the suspect's name up with the chief police spokesperson's name somewhere in the middle. That cost me the only Page 1 correction of my career. But not my job.

And what about crises? Those are actually good days in most newsrooms. They're called "swarm stories," cause for the rallying cry of "all hands on deck." When a scandal rocks a politician, a natural disaster strikes or a crime of awful proportion is committed, a Gulliver-sized man has bitten a Digby-sized dog. Multiple stories must be reported from multiple angles, and everybody jumps in to ensure it's done thoroughly and better than the competition. I used to say during my own days carrying a PRESS card in my wallet that the only time the disparate personalities in the newsroom all meshed in perfect harmony was when there was a crisis to be covered. Or an election. Which is a crisis of sorts to half the populace that didn't vote for the winning candidate or party.

Things can get far tougher, and messier, on the PR side of mistakes and crises. For starters, you can be facing two different kinds of mistakes: the kind you make and the kind discussed above that the journalist makes. Both require the record be set straight in some fashion, and it's nearly impossible to do it yourself. Just like you need a news outlet to commit news, you need one to correct news—whether you misspoke or the journalist misreported. And crises? They always start out for the PR person and his/her client as falling somewhere along the spectrum between annoying/unfortunate and devastating/why not just crawl back into bed? Depending on how quickly and well they're handled, though, they may turn into a chance not just to survive the immediate moment, but to thrive in the next. As John F. Kennedy said while running for president, "In the Chinese language, the word 'crisis' is composed of two characters, one representing danger and the other, opportunity."[63] And JFK knew a thing or two about crises.

BOBBLES, MANGLES AND MISDEEDS

I'm not sure how long you've been reading this book in a single stretch, but even if you just picked it up to dive into Chapter 7 a few minutes ago, why not take a moment to stretch your legs (provided you're not on a plane and the fasten-seatbelts sign is lit)? Get up and take a stroll. Clear any cobwebs that might hinder your comprehension and recall of the topics we're about to cover. And—this is vital—in your moving about find a mirror. Look into it and take a mental snapshot of the face looking

> **You will say or do something you wish you didn't say or do sometime. You're going to try to ROAR, and you're going to wheeze instead.**

back at you. I've not made many guarantees in these pages so far, but I will make one now: That face looking back at you belongs to a person who, if he or she ventures into the mediasphere, will in his or her quest to make news that matters also make something else. A mistake. No ifs, ands, buts or no-way-not-me's about it. You will say or do something you wish you didn't say or do sometime along the path of—don't make the mistake now of not saying it with me—leveraging expectations and opportunities through strategically crafted and applied public relations. You're going to try to ROAR, and you're going to wheeze instead.

Spirit uplifter: You'll have plenty of company, like:

- Gerald Ratner, scion of the family jewelry company now known as the Signet Group, which owns the jingle-earworm retail outlet Kay Jewelers, who in 1991 explained how his firm was able to keep turning a profit during a recession by selling at such affordable prices: "Because it's cheap crap," he said of his merchandise.[64]

- Tony Heyward, former CEO of the BP oil and gas conglomerate, responding to a reporter's question about what he was thinking in the wake of the sinking of his company's Deepwater Horizon oil platform, which resulted in 11 deaths and 4.9 million barrels of oil leaked, the worst spill of its kind in US history: "I want my life back."[65]

- Sean Spicer, President Trump's first press secretary, who was savagely criticized by many in the press in 2017 for his brusque style and sometimes less-than-iron-grip on the facts, who compared Syria's totalitarian regime unfavorably to Nazi Germany, saying "Hitler didn't even sink to using chemical weapons" on his own people.[66]

- And, just for inappropriate grins, whoever handled the Twitter account for our friend, man-bites-dog success story singer Susan Boyle from the book's introduction, who hashtagged an event in which the artist would be releasing her new album with this unfortunate word jumble: #susanalbumparty.[67]

You get the point. When there's a notebook, microphone and/or camera in front of you, sometimes the best thing, or the right thing, doesn't come out of your mouth. Most of the time, it's going to be the innocent remark you don't even realize you said, and certainly didn't mean in the way it sounds. Your intent, unfortunately, does not mitigate potential impact; it doesn't matter that your heart's in the right place if your lips say the wrong thing. Consider my client, a Midwest entertainment company that put on a community festival in 2017 featuring several stages of cover bands performing over a weekend in late July. The gig, called Tribute Island and built around a *Survivor* theme that featured a personal appearance by the show's most (in)famous winner, Richard Hatch, was such a huge success it earned front-page coverage from the local paper. In the story, one of the organizers not trained to speak to the press, because our plan was not to have this person speak to the press, bumped into the reporter (they knew each other socially.)

Our team member remarked, in his glee for what the future could hold for the event as an annual undertaking, that next year it was going to be even better because "we're hoping to … bring on more nationwide, top-of-the-line tribute bands."[68] That quote was certainly not music to the ears of the nearly 40 bands from the region that

An Immunity Idol would have come in handy when a client's hugely
successful 2017 summer festival featuring cover bands
and *Survivor*'s notorious Richard Hatch was nearly undone by a
mistake in one of the quotes our team provided to local media.
(Personal photo.)

entertained thousands. It probably didn't make the fans themselves feel great either, perhaps making them think they paid to see a substandard show. I did my best when I talked to the reporter later that day to course correct, offering simply that, "When you put out a quality event, you get a quality turnout."[69] That ended up being the first quote in the story, creating enough of an upbeat impression from the get-go that it cancelled out the slight downer of the latter quote. We decided no further action was needed to minimize the mistake.

That's not always the case, though. A more assertive approach is often needed to dampen the effects of an error—whether it's committed by the journalist or by you. Bobbles, mangles and misdeeds are indeed survivable, but you can't just wait to be rescued. You have to save yourself. Because, P.T. Barnum's snappy aphorism aside, there is such a thing as bad publicity. It must be eradicated, or at least counterbalanced, as fast as a speeding bullet and with more power than a locomotive (see, I told you I loved Superman.) The three best ways to do that? 1) Reaching out to the reporter off the record; 2) Seeking opportunity to correct the record; and 3) Training like Rocky in one of those "Gonna Fly Now" montage scenes before the big fight so you're better prepared the next time you step into the newsmaking ring.

MAKE IT RIGHT, RIGHT AWAY

Remember our discussion of the 2008 presidential election last chapter? Well, John McCain wasn't the only Republican seeking the GOP nomination that my boss, Dr. James Dobson, was less than impressed with. In part because prominent Christian influencers like Dr. Dobson were not enamored of McCain, former US Sen. (and *Die Hard 2* actor) Fred Thompson jumped into the fray late in primary season, positioning himself as a worthy alternative to the rest of the field that was not exciting voters of faith. But Dr. Dobson wasn't swayed. Per *U.S. News & World Report*:

> 'Everyone knows he's conservative and has come out strongly for the things that the pro-family movement stands

for,' Dobson said of Thompson. '[But] I don't think he's a Christian; at least that's my impression,' Dobson added, saying that such an impression would make it difficult for Thompson to connect with the Republican Party's conservative Christian base and win the GOP nomination.[70]

The reporter Dr. Dobson spoke to, Dan Gilgoff, was/is a good one. He wanted confirmation of the not-a-Christian quote, to make sure it wasn't a slip of the tongue, so he called Dr. Dobson's PR guy. Me. My phone rang, Dan said "hi" and we exchanged pleasantries, then he asked me straight-up-no-chaser if Dr. Dobson had meant to say what he said. My response made headlines for the next few days and still taunts me from the Internet whenever I type my name and the late Sen. Thompson's into Google.

> In a follow-up phone conversation, Focus on the Family spokesman Gary Schneeberger stood by Dobson's claim. He said that, while Dobson didn't believe Thompson to be a member of a non-Christian faith, Dobson nevertheless 'has never known Thompson to be a committed Christian— someone who talks openly about his faith.'

> 'We use that word—Christian—to refer to people who are evangelical Christians,' Schneeberger added. 'Dr. Dobson wasn't expressing a personal opinion about his reaction to a Thompson candidacy; he was trying to 'read the tea leaves' about such a possibility.'[71]

Oh, boy.

There are, as analysts note during football games, multiple flags on that play. My most obvious mistake here was that I didn't stop at confirming what my boss said. I added to it, quite shoddily, in this case defining "Christian" in a way that eliminated, for starters, Catholics from the family of God. As a spokesman for an organization that intentionally stayed out of denominational squabbles and theological debates, I had just started one. Not because I had intentionally decided it was the news

> **I spoke when I should have paused; I wasn't prepared for the question being asked of me, so I had no business responding to it until I was.**

I wanted to commit that day. Not because it advanced the organizational goals of Focus on the Family or the interests of Dr. Dobson. I did it because I spoke when I should have paused; I wasn't prepared for the question being asked of me, so I had no business responding to it until I was.

See, the part of the story I haven't told you yet is that Dr. Dobson's comments to Dan Gilgoff didn't come from a formal interview. They came from Dr. Dobson calling Dan to congratulate him on the success of his new book, which was in large part about Focus. I didn't even know the two had spoken that day, let alone discussed Fred Thompson's faith or lack thereof. The first I heard that Dr. Dobson believed the former senator might not be a Christian was when Dan asked me the question. I should have answered, "That's a great question, Dan. Let me talk with Dr. Dobson to make sure what he said captured everything he wanted to convey, and I'll get back to you." That would have given me time to discuss the issue with Dr. Dobson, to pack the not-a-Christian comment in some ice-cold strategy (like did he *really* want to say it?) and get back to Dan with a comment that would have represented thoughtful, artful framing.

I couldn't take the mistake back now, though. And I had to correct it. I apologized to Dr. Dobson for not checking with him before not just confirming, but augmenting, something I didn't even know for certain he'd said. I told him he counted on me to be more conscientious and complete in my service to him than that, and said I hoped he would continue to trust me moving forward with the important task of helping him make news that mattered. Publicly, we issued a clarifying statement in which we said Dr. Dobson was "attempting to highlight that to the best of his knowledge, Sen. Thompson hadn't clearly

PR-VERB

THE SECOND YOU THINK YOU'VE GOT IT ALL FIGURED OUT ...

I talked at length in Chapter 6 about the myriad ways in which we committed news at Focus on the Family in 2010 with our Tim Tebow Super Bowl ad. The incident here, mercifully, was not part of that news.

That's because, mercifully, it never aired. It was only preserved by the in-house recording equipment in our satellite TV studio at Focus. CBS, the network that conducted the interview, didn't broadcast this segment of it. Mercifully.

I'm not going to describe it here, just set it up. The voice you hear that isn't mine is being piped into my earpiece, and belongs to a producer at the network. Without additional ado, watch my most embarrassing professional moment at the link below. If it doesn't convince you $#!+ is survivable, I got nothing else.

Mercifully.

www.bit.ly/BiteTheDog

communicated his religious faith, and many evangelical Christians might find this a barrier to supporting him."[72] The statement added that Dr. Dobson indicated he had never met Thompson and wasn't sure his impressions of his faith were accurate. "Unfortunately, these qualifiers weren't reported by Mr. Gilgoff."[73] The statement was picked up in a couple of places, but came nowhere near to generating the buzz of the original story.

And I still needed to atone for my mistake to Dan. He had come to me to confirm Dr. Dobson's original statement, and I let him down as well as Dr. Dobson by just winging it rather than researching it. Had I not stumbled forward with an uninformed answer, I could have spared Dan the scrutiny that came with Dr. Dobson saying he was incompletely quoted. I told him I knew he was a fair and thorough reporter. I told him that while I wasn't on the phone with him and Dr. Dobson and had no idea what was said (then qualified or amplified), I knew he wouldn't intentionally make a source look bad by gerrymandering facts. I told him I respected him and hoped he'd trust me in the future to do better by him as a source he relied on for complete and accurate information. I asked for his forgiveness. Dan was, as always, gracious (as was Dr. Dobson.) I kept my job, and I kept my solid working relationship with one of the key reporters through whom I secured coverage that advanced the message and goals of my employer. It remains the best example I have of 1) above—reaching out to a reporter off the record to correct a mistake.

You noticed, I'm sure, there was a whiff of 2) in that last story— seeking opportunity to correct the record. That's why we issued the clarifying statement to frame Dr. Dobson's comments the way I, frankly, should have done in the first place. Far more common in such cases, though, is setting things straight when the mistake is 100 percent on the reporter. I've already said in these pages—gone on the record, if you will—that I believe the vast majority of journalists you'll encounter in the mediasphere are honest and not out to get you. Rarely will they make up facts to intentionally make you look bad; more commonly, they may misinterpret facts that create an impression about you that isn't accurate. That's when, and why, you ask for equal time to realign reality for their readers, listeners or viewers. Sometimes that leads to a follow-up story, sometimes a correction.

That's what we did, again during that ever-spinning newsmaking gerbil's wheel that was Decision 2008, when Focus on the Family's neighbor paper, *The Denver Post*, published an item claiming Dr. Dobson, fed up with the lack of family-values candidates running for president, had proposed "abandoning the GOP and forming a third party that is more distinctly Christian in orientation."[74] It was flatly untrue, and needed to be swept up and tossed away as quickly and concisely as possible. Time to call on our old friend from Chapter 4, the letter to the editor. I wrote and rifled off one that said, in part, "At no point ... has Dr. Dobson said he wants to start, or will cooperate with the start of, a third political party. He has simply encouraged others to consider a principle-based candidate selection strategy come election time, even if that means voting for someone outside the mainstream."[75] Record, corrected.

That doesn't mean, of course, that everybody who saw the mistaken piece also saw the corrected one. But it did provide critical evidence for us when we needed to confront the notion that Dr. Dobson was going to start a third party when it came up again. The reason you want to act as quickly as possible to set straight mistakes by journalists that create a misguided impression of you is so you have such evidence to point to if someone repeats the misguided information. Setting the record straight doesn't necessarily mean everybody who heard the bad information hears the good information. It only means the good information is out there for you to direct audiences to when the bad information pops up again. It's sort of like a game of PR whack-a-mole.

THE 4X4 WILL GET YOU WHERE YOU'RE GOING

Mistakes may be inevitable as you traverse the mediasphere, particularly if you're committing cargo holds of news, but that's no excuse not to shoot for zero tolerance. One of the first things I discuss with new clients, in fact, is how to inoculate themselves against bobbles, mangles and misdeeds. The chief medicine in the

The ROAR 4x4. Don't leave home without it.
(Personal photo.)

shot? *The ROAR 4x4*, a business-card-sized tip sheet—four ideas each for readying and delivering your message in an interview—to help ensure they're prepared to make news that matters. No, the *4x4* does not replace dedicated and detailed media training with a PR coach as discussed in Chapter 4. That remains a critical piece in the Jenga build that is a proper public relations infrastructure; without it, everything will come tumbling down eventually. I share the contents of the *4x4* with you here, though, in the hopes it reinforces not just the need to be prepared for interviews, but the benefit of that preparation when it comes to being heard. And if you want a few copies of the genuine article, hit us up at info@weroar.la.

4 Tips to Ready Your Message

- What's the one point you want to make? *Write it down*. Three ways—25, 15 and 5 words. This may be all you have time for—know it well.

- Be intentional about phrasing: Don't just talk about what you do and believe; talk about how what you do and believe makes a difference.

- Prepare three anecdotes to illustrate the impact of and/or need for your ideas, products and programs. *Speak whenever possible in stories, not statements. They are more moving and persuasive.*

- Practice. Do a mock interview with a colleague or friend. Role play in the mirror. It's not about memorizing lines to parrot, but knowing your talking points well enough that they flow easily and authoritatively.

4 Tips to Deliver Your Message

- *Don't be nervous.* The reporter isn't in charge of the interview; you are. Without you, he or she has no story. You're there to serve your agenda.

- Execute the *bump-and-run*: Acknowledge (bump) the question if it doesn't naturally lead to your talking points, then deliver (run) those talking points (e.g., "That's an interesting question, but I think the real issue is ..."; "I've heard that, but what's really happening is ..."; "That's one way to look at it, but it's more accurate to say ...")

- Smile, even if it's not a TV or video interview. Your tone will reflect it.

- Review your performance. Read, listen to or watch the piece. Note what you want to repeat and improve. Then do it next time.

CRISIS MAKES THE HEART BEAT FASTER

I referred back in Chapter 6 to a media firestorm being "like something out of an Irwin Allen movie." That allusion may have gone over the heads of some readers, like a few others I've sprinkled throughout because I just can't help myself as a child enslaved to '70s and '80s pop culture. For those who don't know, Allen was a film producer nicknamed the "Master of Disaster" for ushering in Hollywood's 1970s fascination with the disaster movie, a genre that visited a natural

(*Earthquake, The Poseidon Adventure*) or man-made (*The Towering Inferno*, the four *Airport* sagas) calamity upon an all-star cast of the era's biggest stars. A good deal of the fun of such pictures, aside from the grand scale and state-of-the-art-at-the-time special effects, was trying to guess which A-list Oscar winner slumming it for a hefty payday would survive the torrents of peril till the credits rolled.

PR crises can feel a lot like you're Paul Newman or Charlton Heston, Faye Dunaway or Ava Gardner, inside your very own disaster movie. They tend to appear and upset your life's apple cart without warning, sometimes set in motion by external forces, sometimes internal ones. They are rife with moments that make your heart race, situations where if you make the right decision you're safe and the wrong one you're doomed, and times you're hit with the very real (figurative) feeling that you won't get out alive. Just as every disaster film features a leader who rises from the ranks of initial survivors to lead those who hang on to ultimate safety, your chances of emerging from the rubble, ashes or water of your crisis rise exponentially if you have a public-relations professional as your guide.

Each crisis is different, of course, but most require two levels of engagement:

- *Identification and assessment.* This is where you find out what's wrong and how bad it is. It's your information-gathering stage, and time is a precious commodity, measured in minutes and hours, not days and weeks. As many hands as you can call to the deck need to be brought together to determine what happened and how it happened. You need to know who's affected; is this only a problem for your brand/organization's reputation, or has genuine harm been caused to your consumers and clients and/or the public? You need to get a grasp on whether the incident responsible for the crisis is internal: Did you or someone associated with you misspeak or misbehave, committing the kind of news you don't want to commit? Or have external factors like product malfunction or cavalcades of criticism dented the goodwill you've worked so hard to build in the marketplace of ideas?

This is also the stage at which you need to decide if you're going to do anything about it. Read that last sentence carefully. This isn't the time you decide *what* you're going to do to confront and clear up the crisis. It's when you decide *if* you're going to do anything proactive to confront and clear up the crisis. Remember what I said about the 24-hour news cycle breeding short memories? You may decide the best strategy is to offer no response, to let tomorrow's headlines wipe away today's. Doing so, doing nothing, is always a calculated risk. Depending on the severity of the crisis, and the tentacles that could grow from it like a Hydra's heads and extend or deepen the crisis with more unfavorable news stories, silence may be the golden decision. If it's not, though, you need to stop thinking and start doing.

- *Response, not reaction.* If you decide to speak up and out in an effort to mitigate the crisis, to douse it down to its embers so it has no chance of conflagrating again, you're going to need a strategy. Everything we've talked about to this point about effective PR being the—scream it like you're an extra in a disaster movie!—wise leveraging of expectations and opportunities applies to crisis communications, too. Even more so. The worst thing you can do is rush out a comment that's only been half thought-through. That's a *reaction*; you need a *response*. It must address the source of the crisis, acknowledge your or your allies' role in it and propose what you'll do to drop the situation back down below DEFCON 3. By now the initial hours of the crisis will have unfurled, but you're still working in terms of hours and days. Implementing and carrying out your response—if it involves a recall or cleanup from a man-made disaster like an oil spill, for instance—is when you start getting into weeks and months territory. Those situations are unlikely to crop up for you as an author, expert, speaker, coach and consultant.

Let's take a little more time unpacking the point above about acknowledging your or your allies' role in the crisis you're dealing with. There's a platinum truth in the execution of this requirement where many crisis responses go south. It's been awhile since I asked you to highlight anything, but get those markers ready again, because you'll want to remember this No. 1 determiner of surviving a crisis: Owning up to a mistake allows you the opportunity to live another day, because it's easier to earn back trust after an error than an untruth. (This, of course, does not apply if you haven't actually made a mistake— if the crisis is of completely outside origin.)

> **Owning up to a mistake allows you the opportunity to live another day, because it's easier to earn back trust after an error than an untruth.**

Look no further than the sexual harassment and assault scandals that erupted like scores of Mount Vesuviuses across the entertainment industry in 2017. Some of those accused as alleged predators hemmed and hawed their ways to Janet Jackson Apologies (see Chapter 6), lawyered up instead of fessing up, and tried to misdirect the media by announcing they were making nebulous trips to rehab and even, in one instance, choosing the moment to come out as gay after four decades of sexual-preference silence in the spotlight. Others, a scant few to be sure, took the more honest and direct approach. Among the most notable of them was comedian Louis C.K., who issued a statement that read, in part, "These stories are true. … There is nothing about this that I forgive myself for. And I have to reconcile it with who I am. Which is nothing compared to the task I left (my victims) with ... The hardest regret to live with is what you've done to hurt someone else."[76]

The comic certainly doesn't deserve the Jean Hersholt Humanitarian Award for acknowledging that he exposed himself to powerless women over a period of several years. Movies and comedy specials he had in the works were cancelled, and rightly so. His manager dumped him, which indicates how toxic even association with him had become. But Louis C.K. does deserve respect on a single front: When the truth came out, he admitted it without qualification. In a statement that, if the coarse words and grammatical errors are an indication, came from his keyboard directly and not a phalanx of lawyers. If anyone tattooed as an abuser as part of that terrible Hollywood crisis has a chance of career resurrection at the proper time, it will be him. I'm not saying it will happen. I'm not saying it should happen. I'm saying it might happen because it is easier to earn back trust after an error, even a horrific one that left multiple victims in its wake, than an untruth that claims you are the victim when there is ample evidence to the contrary.

JERUSALEM, WE HAVE A PROBLEM

When you work in Hollywood, 4 a.m. phone calls the night after one of your TV shows airs are rarely a welcome development. And indeed it was not a welcome development when my phone rang at that hour in Spring 2013, just one sunset after the first episode of *The Bible* that featured Jesus aired. The call was from my boss, but conferenced in were senior marketing executives with HISTORY, which broadcast the miniseries, and Roma Downey and Mark Burnett, who produced it and had been championing it in the media for months. The crisis that awakened me from a sound and satisfied sleep—the miniseries was, after all, tearing up the ratings—involved the introduction of Satan in the previous night's episode. It had nothing to do with how Ol' Scratch was depicted from a theological perspective. We had dealt with a smattering of criticism about biblical accuracy in earlier episodes— Ninja angels!?!—but this was a more cosmetic controversy. It seems social media was blowing up with viewers who thought the The Father of Lies looked like The Leader of the Free World. That's right: We were being accused of intentionally making the devil look like President Barack Obama.

That wasn't true—but it would continue to gather steam as opinion that might metastasize into fact if we didn't launch into crisis-communications mode. Step 1: Investigate and assess. Turns out it all started, at least at a level large numbers of people noticed, with a tweet by conservative talk-show host Glenn Beck (ironically, a fan of the series.) He thumbed out, "Anyone else think the Devil in #TheBible Sunday on History Channel looks exactly like That Guy?"[77] Over the

Does he or doesn't he? The truth is, it doesn't really matter. People thought he did, even though he wasn't intended to. A crisis ensued, and good PR solved it. (*Hollywood Reporter*[78])

course of more than a thousand comments and retweets, the masses were essentially saying President Obama and Mohamen Mehdi Ouazanni, the actor portraying Satan, were something akin to Patty Duke playing identical cousins. And that everyone involved intended the resemblance as a slap at the president.

We determined with zero hesitation that we had to address it. It was not going to go away on its own, and if it lingered it would draw attention away from the show's stratospheric success—one week, the series even outpaced *The Walking Dead* in the Nielsens, prompting glorious man-bites-dog headlines like "God Beats Zombies."[79] More important, it was already and would only continue to siphon viewer focus off the content of the series, especially unfortunate now that it had moved into New Testament tales. This was TV with a purpose, you remember from earlier discussions; the goal was to awaken Americans to the beauty of the Bible in the hopes of leading those who had never picked it up or cracked it open to do so.

So it was decided to refute the comparisons strongly, using good old-fashioned facts (PR-Verb, Chapter 6) to make our case. Roma and Mark issued a take-no-prisoners statement calling the whole kerfuffle "utter nonsense" and noting that Ouazanni "previously played parts in several biblical epics—including Satanic characters long before Barack Obama was elected as our president."[80] It was additionally noted that Mark had donated to President Obama's campaign in 2008 and the Democratic National Committee in 2009.[81] Within a few hours of my phone ringing at 4 a.m., industry trades and major news organizations were updating their stories on Doppelgangergate to lead with Roma and Mark's stern correction of the record. The crisis was gone before the sun was.

In an interesting postscript, though, the issue returned long enough the following year to help draw attention to the theatrical film created from the Jesus portions of the miniseries. It's a perfect story to end this chapter, because it illustrates quite evocatively that not only is $#!+ survivable, but President Kennedy was spot on in his stump speeches in 1959 and '60 when he pointed out the Chinese word for crisis means not only danger, but opportunity. The final cut of *Son of God* included not a frame of footage of Satan, by design, because Downey and Burnett wanted to "give the devil his due"—i.e., nothing. The duo leveraged viewers' memory of the Obama/Satan dustup to commit news that delivered a key message about their hopes for the film: that it would introduce Jesus to a new generation of moviegoers. Heck, it was even man-bites-dog news in the way it upset expectations, since conventional wisdom was that the couple would avoid revisiting the subject of their miniseries' biggest bout with bad press. But Roma hit it head on with an op-ed in *USA Today*, the largest-circulation daily newspaper in the US:

> *The Bible* series was in its third week when Jesus began to appear on the big screen. There was great excitement that Jesus was coming, with our trailers, various talk shows and even Twitter buzzing with anticipation.
>
> He was beautiful and strong and kind and compassionate. His presence uplifted and encouraged people. It was everything we had hoped for.
>
> But there was supernatural opposition at work. The devil was also in that episode. Someone made a comment that the actor who played the devil vaguely resembled our president, and suddenly the media went nuts. It went global, showing up all over TV and the Internet. That next day, when I was sure everyone would only be talking about Jesus, they were talking about Satan instead. …
>
> But for our movie, *Son of God*, I wanted all of the focus to be on Jesus. I want his name to be on the lips of everyone who sees this movie, so we cast Satan out. It gives me great pleasure to tell you that the devil is on the cutting-room floor. This is now a movie about Jesus, the Son of God, and the devil gets no more screen time, no more distractions.[82]

NEXT UP

See that up ahead? It's the finish line—and the starting line. You're almost done with this book; just one chapter left. In it, we're going to recap what we've covered to help you make news that matters. If that seems repetitive, well, that's the nature of consistently committing news that bites the dog. Build the strategy and structure and keep executing the first one through the second. *Voila!* You're a newsmaker.

8

Pitch. Place. Repeat.

Baseball is, if all the aphorisms that have sprung from it are any indication, a metaphor for life. Some of the greatest hitters in the history of the game, the ones so good announcers say they see pitches coming toward them in slow motion, have summed up the science of their swing as nothing more than repetition. Finding a stroke and finding it again and again and again. Attaining that all-too-elusive "groove" announcers also talk about. Those All-Stars are on to something critical about strategically crafted and applied public relations, too.

Good PR, like America's pastime, involves many players on different teams of varying skill levels. Your goal when you step into the mediasphere, or the batter's box, is to get a hit—the most valuable and rewarding kind being a home run. You can't play either game effectively without a coach/manager. Practice doesn't make you perfect, but it makes you better. And, as every baseball Hall of Famer knows, the key to any of it is to do all of it over and over again. The skills ballplayers learn in Little League are the ones they still repeat in the Major Leagues. And so it is for you: The tactics we've discussed in this book will continue to yield results if you don't stop at merely applying them once. You have to apply them repeatedly.

RERELEVANCE ISN'T A WORD, BUT LET'S MAKE IT ONE

PR is, I hope I've shown throughout this book, more art than science. But if we could distill down into a formula what strategically crafted and applied public relations that can buttress your brand and amplify your message is, it might look something like this:

$$\textbf{Identity + Strategy + Opportunity x Achievement}^{\textbf{Resilience}} \textbf{= Relevance}$$

That's the endgame. Relevance. You don't approach the media-asphere dressed in one of Steven Seagal's signature 17-button dusters unless what you're aiming for is relevance. Because it's the relevant brands—the relevant authors, experts, speakers, coaches and consultants—that the press pays attention to. And do you know the easiest way to get them to pay attention to you more than once? Be relevant more than once. Be—we'll just make up a word here because my fingers are on the keyboard and I can punch any keys in succession I want—*rerelevant*. Make news that matters today. Then do it again tomorrow. Never stop looking for expectations and opportunities to leverage, and you'll never run out of expectations and opportunities to leverage. (I didn't make you say it with me that time because I figured you might be getting hoarse by now, and you'll need your voice for all those interviews you're going to be doing.)

A prime example of this played out in late 2017 with Renaissance Women Productions, an independent, non-profit, faith-based production company and ROAR client that, as its value proposition puts it, "is an incubator for new talent, providing apprenticeship and a chance to then be involved at a higher level on other for-profit productions." We specifically signed on to help them promote an original streaming series, *Daily Bread,*

> **Make news that matters today. Then do it again tomorrow. Never stop looking for expectations and opportunities to leverage, and you'll never run out of expectations and opportunities to leverage.**

The dramatic streaming series *Daily Bread* is a solid case study in rerelevance. It made news in two distinct ways: first for its unique take on tales of a dystopian future and second for its production company's status as an alternative for young talent not quite ready to make it in Hollywood. (Photo courtesy Renaissance Women Productions.)

that chronicles life in a post-apocalyptic America flung back to the Dark Ages by a solar flare that turns off the electricity worldwide—forever. We generated some solid coverage on the content of the show itself, spotlighting its slightly different take on the dystopian fiction genre. As talk show host and former Arkansas Gov. Mike Huckabee put it in a succinct way that makes me envious: "It's like *The Hunger Games*, if the hunger was for God's righteousness and holding on to our humanity even when times are bleak."[83]

Because we had an infrastructure and strategy in place to identify and act on news developments where Renaissance Women's voice could add to the conversation, we developed an entirely different pitch when Hollywood's sexual misconduct crisis hit. As word spread of producing kingpin Harvey Weinstein, then other power brokers from director Brett Ratner to actor Kevin Spacey, being accused of terrible, even criminal acts of impropriety, we knew we had a chance to make more news that mattered. Renaissance Women Productions, you see, had been started more than 10 years prior as a safe place for young performers in front of and behind the camera to get some credits on their IMDb profile without having to subject themselves to the vulgarities and vagaries of Hollywood. So we offered founder Nina May, who was also the creator and director of *Daily Bread*, as someone who could spotlight that there was another, better way for those who felt called to the performing arts to jumpstart their careers. That the core cast of the series were young women—the primary victims in the Weinstein et al. outrage—only made the story that much more appealing to the press.

"We launched Renaissance Women Productions because there were so many young women who wanted to work in the industry, but who were not comfortable with the Hollywood dynamic, where they were afraid they would have to compromise their integrity just to get a job," Nina said in one interview. "Renaissance Women Productions is a faith-based organization where people are safe. They can express their opinion on faith or conservative politics without fear of occupational reprisal. Everyone here is able to learn and expand their craft without judgment."[84]

Another outlet wanted to hear from one of the actresses herself.

"After just four years as a professional actress, Gabriella Kostadi-nova, who plays Nora on the TV series, says she has 'brushed shoul-ders' with producers and directors who acted inappropriately," One News Now reported. "She (says) coming to the set of *Daily Bread* was like a breath of fresh air. Each day starts with prayer, she says, there is no cursing on the set, the cast is a like a close-knit family, and the wardrobes are modest."[85]

Similar commitment to rerelevance has guided ROAR's work with Brad Kullman, the former Major League Baseball executive whose initial splash after joining the ROAR roster was an op-ed in *The Washington Post* (Chapter 5) decrying the epidemic in pro sports of teams "tanking for titles." Brad has the pedigree and the passion to confront this problem of teams intentionally fielding subpar lineups today in the hope of losing enough now to potentially win a championship later. The great thing about having "put the compete back in big-league competition" as your calling card is that it's always somebody's sports season—so there will always be opportunities to turn today's headlines that don't feature you into tomorrow's that do. It also always offers a chance to bite the dog because fans of bottom-tier teams have been shammed into believing the only way to claim the crown is to throw in the towel several seasons running. Brad comes along and those poor bowsers don't know what bit them.

Most-recent-as-of-this-writing case in point: In December 2017, the New York Giants benched two-time Super Bowl-winning quarterback Eli Manning the week after they were eliminated from playoff contention, saying all the usual things tankers say about wanting to "get a look at" less experienced players in "planning for the future." Brad saw it for what it was, though, and we quickly hit New York and New Jersey sports talk radio—where opinions go to be expressed thermonuclearly—offering him as a guest to counterbalance those voices who might be thankful that no Eli meant more losing, which would mean a higher draft pick and potential future superstar. Brad landed on WNYU Radio to discuss it and assert his rerelevance.

HERE'S THE WINDUP AND THE ...

Everybody knows rerelevance requires a delivery mechanism. OK, no they don't. Nobody even knew what rerelevance was till I made the word up at the start of this chapter. But it does occur to me there's one final bit of counsel I need to offer you in your quest to make news that matters, and to make it repetitively. You have to know how to pitch—and it's not as simple as just raring back and firing. You need finesse more than a fastball if you're going to—c'mon, just one more time?—leverage the expectations and opportunities in the mediasphere to become rerelevant. And finesse in this case means knowing the pros and cons of each pitch format.

'NO COMMENT' IS A BAD COMMENT

I began these PR-Verbs with an interview tip: Just do them. Because you, not the reporter, are always in charge. "Without the things you have to say to populate their story, they have no story," I wrote. "They have the ability to ask the questions, yes, but ... you have the ability to a) answer those questions or not; and, most importantly, b) decide how to answer them."

Let's finish, then, with a tip on answering those questions right. First, never say "No comment." It is, in fact, a comment, the worst answer you can give because it makes you seem like you have something to hide. Instead of refusing to answer, respond in a way that signals you're aware of what the interviewer is after even as you provide him or her the information you prepared to deliver to ensure your message hits its mark.

The best way to do this is what I referenced in *The Roar 4x4* (Chapter 7) as the bump-and-run. Acknowledge (bump) the question, then deliver (run) your talking points. Like this:

Interviewer: Some people have said you've lost your influence. That you don't have the clout you once had. Are they right?

You: I've heard that, too, but the truth is we're as active and involved on a global scale as we've ever been, with sales showing growth in the key demographics we're aiming for.

The power lies in the pivot of "I've heard that, too." Other options, depending on the details of the question, are "That's an interesting question, but I think the real issue is ..." and "That's one way to look at it, but it's more accurate to say ..." In each case, you can't be accused of dodging the question because you're making very clear you've heard it; you're just indicating you don't think it's a valid question and offering an answer that better addresses the issue at hand.

Good reporters, it should be noted, will recognize the bump-and-run and rephrase and re-ask the question they want to pin back your ears with. Always remember, you can execute the bump-and-run every time—just mix up the words and phrases so as not to sound like a robot.

Let's start with the …

Interview Availability—Exhibit A

Pros: Pithy. Never more than a page. No room for pushing multiple story angles or the Dickensian flourishes a writer may fall victim to (guilty!) when penning/keyboarding one of the other two pitch types. It's just-the-facts-ma'am, a single-focus rundown of who is available, why he or she is available, and why the journalist should care. Speaking of the journalist, another pro is that experience tells me more of them will actually read your interview availability as opposed to your more involved pitches. You may argue whether brevity is truly the soul of wit, but there's no argument it's more effective at capturing a busy reporter's or producer's attention.

Cons: Works best when what you want covered isn't a thing, but a person. And a person the journalist will know just by reading the name. Yes, you need to offer at least a few bits of bio to round out the recipient's knowledge, but in general this pitch should be reserved for someone who's achieved a certain level of cultural profile.

In Exhibit A, that person is Richard Hatch, the inaugural *Survivor* winner who parlayed his fame from that show into a nice little career as a reality-TV mainstay. Hatch, as you'll recall from the previous chapter, did a personal appearance at an event one of our clients held. He was not the main draw—cover bands, remember?—but was the biggest name. So the strategy was to use his fame, only augmented since *Survivor* by the public twists and turns of his life, to hook the media to get his story. He was gracious enough, then, to mention the event in the course of the interviews we secured. The story wound up being about more than him but came to be because of him.

News Advisory—Exhibit B

Pros: Opportunity to serve up complex or multiple story angles and still keep the length manageable—one page is the goal but some spill to a second isn't the worst thing that could happen. This is your best option when you have to introduce and connect several concepts that need to be understood in context. It also gives you more room to describe products and services that are unique to the value proposition of the client. And, maybe it's just me, but "news advisory" arrests the reader's attention a little better than "press release." Nothing but instinct to back it up, but I think that equates to a few more clicks-to-open.

Cons: Can wind up awfully dense with text, which is a turnoff to reading once it is open. It tends to be factual text, too, and such a thick soup of details can be harder to digest. News advisories often come across as overstuffed—too much information crammed into too restrictive a format.

Exhibit B has an interesting history. It was initially distributed to national sports digital and broadcast media the morning after the Houston Astros won the 2017 World Series. The strategy was since the Astros had tanked their way to a title a year after the Chicago Cubs did the same, there would be a lot of people won over to the argument that it's the best way for a team to conduct a "rebuilding process." Brad Kullman and I, in fact, even though we had no dog in the hunt in terms of clubs we rooted for, were pulling mightily for the Astros because it would trigger more relevance for our pitch. And then ... nothing.

But a few days later, *The Washington Post* columnist who said the Green Bay Packers should tank published his piece. I tweaked the intro to the original news advisory to refer to that piece, left the rest pretty much intact and reached out to editors at *The Post*. They bit quickly to commission Brad's op-ed. He had committed news.

Press Release—Exhibit C

Pros: It allows you the most creative leeway and latitude in describing the brand distinctives you want the media to cover. Because it is, at least in its best application, written like a news story, there is the possibility—however slim—a print or digital outlet will publish it in its entirety. (Please note: If this happens, it will not happen in *The New York Times*. It will happen in a publication of less journalistic ambition, most commonly one that engages in directed reporting or represents old-school industry and hobby media discussed in Chapter 2.) A press release is the only pitch that really allows you to include quotes from yourself about the products or services you're pitching.

Cons: Start with my PR-Verb on Chapter 5. To that I would add that a press release really isn't an awareness or coverage-generating tool. It's best used internally—as a post on your website, for instance, offering the kind of depth and breadth those who are already your clients and customers will find useful. That's why industry custom requires appending a biography of the individual(s) or organizations(s) the release is about. That takes up even more room and likely leads to even fewer readers among journalists.

The press release in Exhibit C was done for precisely the purpose mentioned above. We wanted a one-stop summary of the rhyme and reason behind *Daily Bread* for posting on the series' website. I also sent the release to reporters *after* I secured coverage via another tactic to give them a full summary of the show's themes, plot, producers, etc.

Two final 30,000-foot-level thoughts on pitches. First, I cannot discourage you more—unless maybe I had a cue ball wrapped in a bar towel—if you're tempted to pay to post any type of pitch on one of those online "wire services." The price is exorbitant for what you get: a link to something precious few journalists will ever see, let alone read.

You are far better off personally pitching—through your designated PR coach, of course. And that's where Point No. 2 comes into play. As we've discovered in our discussion of creating infrastructure and executing strategy, you'll need someone besides yourself to be responsible for reaching out to and building relationships with the reporters, editors, hosts and producers whose megaphones you need to reach the masses. The first thing a good coach will/should tell you is any pitch strategy is doomed to fail if it relies on blindly blasting news outlets rather than investing time in microtargeting and personally reaching out to the right people at the right news outlets. And they can't be afraid to pick up the phone, either.

OK, here are the exhibits we've just discussed. Give them a look but come back when you're done. I've got one last thought to leave you with.

Exhibit A – Interview Availability

Interview Availability

Contact:
Gary Schneeberger
gary@weroar.la / 818-309-8580

7-10-17

Schedule Your Interview Today with SURVIVOR'S First and Most Notorious Winner, Richard Hatch

Will appear July 22-23 at Tribute Island on Kenosha's lakefront; music fest features 36 cover bands from across Ill. and Wis.

KENOSHA, Wis. – Richard Hatch, the first and still most celebrated winner of the CBS reality series SURVIVOR, is available for interviews in advance of his appearance July 22-23 at TRIBUTE ISLAND, a first-of-its-kind music festival on Kenosha's lakefront.

The event will feature 36 of the most celebrated tribute acts from across the Midwest playing a wide variety of the most popular music of the last half century. More information, including the festival lineup, can be found at www.tributeisland.com.

Hatch emerged victorious during the inaugural season of the megahit SURVIVOR, earning a reputation as reality TV's first villain and fame he has parlayed over the last 17 years into numerous television appearances on shows such as THE CELEBRITY APPRENTICE (hosted by Donald Trump), THE BIGGEST LOSER and WHO WANTS TO BE A MILLIONAIRE. He will sign autographs and take pictures with fans at the event.

He is available immediately for telephone and satellite interviews to discuss his reality show experiences and Tribute Island.

Who: SURVIVOR winner Richard Hatch

What: Tribute Island

Where: Simmons Island, Kenosha

When: Event is July 22-23; interview availability is immediate and ongoing

Why You Should Cover: Hatch defined how to win a competition reality show – and he has many insights into what makes such shows successful. He also can offer free-wheeling anecdotes about working with now-President Donald Trump when they both starred on THE CELEBRITY APPRENTICE.

www.weroar.la

Exhibit B – News Advisory

ROAR
Contact: Gary Schneeberger
gary@weroar.is
818-309-9580

News Advisory

BRAD KULLMAN

Losing (To Win)

How Incentivized Losing
Undermines the Integrity of Our
Major Professional Sports Leagues

Nov. 2, 2017

Astros, Cubs World Series Wins Portend Tanking Epidemic

Fans all over southeast Texas are ecstatic right now, basking in the thrill that their Astros are World Series champs, their first title in franchise history. Chicago Cubs fans have similarly spent the past year celebrating their team's historic breaking of a 108-year championship drought. This happy occasion for fans, though, is about to set off an outbreak of "tanking" that could signal the end of baseball, and major league professional sports, as we've always known and appreciated them, according to former Cincinnati Reds General Manager Brad Kullman.

That's because both the Astros and Cubs built their impressive rosters while consciously not trying to win over several seasons. Houston lost at least 106 games each year from 2011 to 2013, blatantly fielding non-competitive teams while focusing solely on stockpiling minor league prospects and high draft picks that became the eventual stars of this year's squad. Ditto the Cubs, whose head of baseball operations, Theo Epstein, has conspicuously bragged that his team's road to the top was paved with "not letting our competitiveness overwhelm our objectivity." Translation: They tanked today, in hopes of winning a title tomorrow.

Kullman, a former MLB scout and front-office executive who was an early proponent of sabermetrics, foresees a "tanking epidemic" as teams rush to imitate the blueprint laid by the two most recent World Series champs. He forecasts a widening chasm between the "haves" (who are trying to compete) and the "have-nots" (who are "rebuilding"). The rules that allow this, he says, amount to "a broken welfare system that effectively exploits teams and is unwittingly celebrated by fans and the media." In his book, *Losing (To Win): How Incentivized Losing Undermines the Integrity of Our Major Professional Sports Leagues,* he doesn't simply call out tanking for the "toxic environment" it is; a handful of analysts, to their credit, have also done that. Kullman goes a big step further, presenting a bold blueprint for revising draft processes in a way that will not only enhance competitive balance, but restore respect for winning and put the "compete" back in major league sports competition.

www.weroar.is

Exhibit C – Press Release

Press Release

Contact Gary Schneeberger
gary@weroar.la
818-309-8580

|

FOR IMMEDIATE RELEASE / Aug. XX 2017

Action-Packed New Streaming Series
Imagines a World Gone Dark ...
and How the Good Book and a Cookbook
Help Those Struggling to Survive
Hold on to Their Humanity

*DAILY BREAD, a story that may yet
be ripped from the headlines, to premiere Sept. 8,
certain to appeal to viewers who love God, guns and girls*

People from all walks of life, with all levels of faith in God and government, must search for something to hold onto when they lose their grip on everything they're known in DAILY BREAD, a faith-based, post-apocalyptic new streaming series launching its first season Sept. 8.

When a solar flare knocks out electricity everywhere and forever, life changes in an instant for friends, families and total strangers who find themselves bound together in rebuilding their lives without the modern conveniences and luxuries society has taken for granted for generations. Their safety, and in some cases their sanity, are threatened as they take their tentative first steps into this brave new world only a few of them ever deemed possible.

Exhibit C – Press Release (continued)

"If you like God, guns and girls, this show is for you," says creator/writer/director Nina May, who produced the series through her Renaissance Women Productions. "There's plenty of entertainment and excitement here, but also many 'What if?' moments for viewers. Especially when we look at headlines about potential conflicts with foreign countries who hate our way of life, we want viewers to realize such a thing really could happen. We want them to go on this journey with our characters and put themselves in the place of the people they see on the screen.

"This is not a show to be watched passively," she adds. "If we've done our job right, the action and the themes will make you think a little bit, too."

To that end, there are characters just about everyone can identify with. At the center of the action are "The Foodies," the cast and crew of a popular cooking show hosted by Tiffany McMillan (Francesca Finnerty), author of the best-seller "Shop Poor, Eat Rich." Her two sisters, Sophie (Sheila Ayelino) and Nora (Gabriella Kostadinova) work with her, along with a talented and tenacious group of millennial women. Like The Foodies, also taken by surprise by the solar flare are "The Posse," guests at a hotel led by Skylar (NEED NAME), a sheltered young woman who must rise to the occasion to build a city from the shelter she and her new acquaintances thought was temporary.

DAILY BREAD also traces the journey of Holly (Sandra Belforte), an uptight attorney who has to turn to her estranged sister, who lives at a camp of rural "preppers" – the only group of characters who expected a catastrophic event like this would happen and who have their own unique trials to overcome as their abstract ideas about post-apocalyptic existence conflict with the reality they are forced to face. There are also high-school students and homeschool families whose efforts to accept the new normal are evocatively depicted.

As the days and weeks of their new lives unfurl, all these characters will intersect in ways tied to Tiffany's cookbook, even as they learn to draw greater strength from another book – the Bible, and the truths of a God whose love and promises don't change an iota when the lights go out.

"Happiness and joy and hope aren't circumstantial when God is your focus," May says. "We can walk through the valley of the shadow of death – or a solar flare that knocks us back to Revolutionary times – and still emerge with our humanity intact."

DAILY BREAD will be released "binge style" – all episodes available at once – on Sept. 8. Information on how and where to view it can be found at https://www.rwpvideo.org/

###

About Renaissance Women Productions

Renaissance Women Productions is a non-profit 501c3 organization and a project of the Renaissance Foundation. We have produced award-winning films, documentaries, TV shows, and shorts for the past 10 years. Our mission is working with new and undiscovered talent, to give them the opportunity to break into the film industry. The students, interns, and enthusiasts that have come through the foundation have produced everything from TV shows, to commercials, documentaries, educational, and even feature films.

www.weroar.la

NEXT UP

I've ended every chapter in this book with a look ahead at what comes next. Now, though, it's not about literally turning the page. It's about figuratively turning it and embarking on your career as a newsmaker. The road ahead of you is not an easy one, but it is a rewarding one. It may not be the straightest, smoothest path, but it is the one that leads to exactly where you want to go. I know that because I made some assumptions about you when we first met all the way back in the introduction. And if you're still reading on the last page, I was right in those assumptions.

"I'm guessing you're holding this book right now because you have something you want to say that you want people to hear," I wrote. "Maybe you think of it as your calling. Maybe it's your job. Maybe it's a message you feel you've been uniquely equipped to share. There's a good chance it's all three. In fact, you're probably already putting that message out there—via a blog, an email list or public-speaking gigs. And yet ... you feel like something's missing. You could/should have a bigger audience, bigger influence, bigger impact. You're not yet achieving your goal, at least not on the level you'd like, to change hearts with what's in your heart. You want more, most likely not just for yourself, but for those who could benefit from what you have to say, and you aren't getting it. Worse, you're not sure how to go about getting it."

"Let's change that."

I hope that's what we've done in our time together. I hope you now feel equipped to become a 7th-dan black belt in the wise leveraging of expectations and opportunities to make news that matters. I hope your deepened understanding of strategically crafted and applied public relations buttresses your brand and amplifies your message.

I hope you bite the dog.

Somebody Besides Me Say Something Now, Please

I've done an inordinate amount of talking/typing here, and I don't know about you, but I'm dying for somebody else to—cue the ROAR brand promise—be heard. Since you're the one who's been gracious enough to invest your time reading the book, I hope it'll be you who speaks up now.

I'd love to know what you think about *Bite the Dog*. What rings true? What do you disagree with? Where would more information be valuable? Are you still confused by those walking-and-talking rock creatures in *Noah*? I'd also love to hear about your experiences in the mediasphere. If you haven't visited it yet, then tell me about your aspirations once you get there.

Whatever your comment or criticism or concern, I'd be honored if you took a minute or two to share it with me. You can shoot an email directly to my inbox: gary@weroar.la.

In the meantime, if you'd like to know more about ROAR's history and the services we offer, stop by our website at **www.weroar.la**. You can even sign up for our email newsletter for tips on continuing to— you guessed it—leverage expectations and opportunities to help you make news that matters.

May every dog you bite be tasty,

149

Endnotes

1 Mark Barna, "Focus leader Jim Daly recovering after motorcycle crash," *Gazette.com*, June 25, 2010, http://gazette.com/focus-leader-jim-daly-recovering-after-motorcycle-crash/article/100786.

2 Ibid.

3 "Susan Boyle - Britain's Got Talent audition, You Tube," *DailyMail.com*, undated, http://www.dailymail.co.uk/video/news/video-12353/Susan-Boyle-Britains-Got-Talent-audition-YouTube.html.

4 Roma Downey and Mark Burnett, "Why Public Schools Should Teach the Bible," *WSJ.com*, March 1, 2013, https://www.wsj.com/articles/SB1000 1424127887324338604578326150289837608.

5 Bruce Feiler, *America's Prophet: Moses and the American Story* (New York: William Morrow, 2009), 35.

6 Robert Wynne, "The Real Difference Between PR And Advertising," *Forbes.com*, July 8, 2014, https://www.forbes.com/sites/robertwynne/2014/07/08/the-real-difference-between-pr-and-advertising-credibility/#42e26f0b2bb9.

7 Claire Daniel, "PR vs. Advertising: Still the Same Competition?" *AdWeek.com*, July 9, 2014, http://www.adweek.com/digital/pr-vs-advertising-still-the-same-competition/.

8 Wynne, "The Real Difference Between PR and Advertising."

9 James Poniewozik, "TV Tonight: Scandal," *Time.com*, April 5, 2012, http://entertainment.time.com/2012/04/05/tv-tonight-scandal/.

10 "Best Buffets in Las Vegas," *Vegas.com*, undated, https://www.vegas.com/traveltips/top-10-buffets/

11 Michael Barthel, "5 key takeaways about the State of the News Media in 2016," *PewResearch.org*, June 15, 2016, http://www.pewresearch.org/fact-tank/2016/06/15/state-of-the-news-media-2016-key-takeaways/.

12 Ibid.

13 Tom Krattenmaker, "What Evangelicals Can Learn From Superman (and Other Secular Culture)," *HuffingtonPost.com*, August 19, 2013, https://www.huffingtonpost.com/tom-krattenmaker/evangelicals-man-of-steel_b_3463152.html.

14   Robinson Meyer, "How Many Stories Do Newspapers Publish Per Day?", *TheAtlantic.com*, May 26, 2016, https://www.theatlantic.com/ technology/archive/2016/05/how-many-stories-do-newspapers-publish-per-day/483845/.

15   "Most Stressful Jobs of 2017," *CareerCast.com*, undated, http://www. careercast.com/jobs-rated/most-stressful-jobs-2017.

16   "Journalism: Statistics & Facts," *Statista.com*, undated, https://www. statista.com/topics/2096/journalism/.

17   Derek Thompson, "Report: Journalists Are Miserable, Liberal, Over-Educated, Under-Paid, Middle-Aged Men," *TheAtlantic.com*, May 8, 2014, https://www.theatlantic.com/business/archive/2014/05/report-journalists-are-miserable-over-educated-under-paid-middle-aged-men-mostly/361891/.

18   "Trump to CNN's Jim Acosta: You're fake news," *CNN.com*, January 11, 2017, http://www.cnn.com/videos/politics/2017/08/14/trump-calls-cnn-fake-news-acosta-sot-mobile.cnn.

19   Izabella Kaminska, "A lesson in fake news from the info-wars of ancient Rome," *FT.com*, January 17, 2018, www.ft.com/content/aaf2bb08-dca2-11e6-86ac-f253db7791c6.

20   "The fake news that sealed the fate of Antony and Cleopatra," *TheConversation.com*, January 13, 2017, http://theconversation.com/the-fake-news-that-sealed-the-fate-of-antony-and-cleopatra-71287.

21   Gregory S. Schneider, "The fake news that haunted George Washington," *WashingtonPost.com*, April 10, 2017, https://www. washingtonpost.com/news/retropolis/wp/2017/04/10/the-fake-news-that-haunted-george-washington/?utm_term=.95863c640b04.

22   Jacob Soll, "The Long and Brutal History of Fake News," *Politico.com*, December 18, 2016, https://www.politico.com/magazine/story/2016/12/ fake-news-history-long-violent-214535.

23   "Madalyn Murray O'Hair Trying to Get References to God Removed from Touched By An Angel and Other TV or Radio Shows-Fiction!", *TruthorFiction.com*, March 17, 2015, https://www.truthorfiction.com/ madelynmurrayohair-touched/.

24   Michael Roberts, "Focus on the Family Action's rebranding as CitizenLink a bid to 'minimize the confusion'," *Westword.com*, May 20, 2010, http://www.westword.com/news/focus-on-the-family-actions-rebranding-as-citizenlink-a-bid-to-minimize-the-confusion-5899244.

25 Maxwell Murphy, "What does value proposition mean in business?", Quora.com, August 27, 2015, https://www.quora.com/What-does-value-proposition-mean-in-business

26 *Cambridge Dictionary Online*, Value Proposition, https://dictionary.cambridge.org/us/dictionary/english/value-proposition

27 "Spin (propaganda)," *Wikipedia.com*, undated, https://en.wikipedia.org/wiki/Spin_(propaganda.)

28 *Oxford English Dictionary Second Edition* on CD-ROM (v. 4.0) © Oxford University Press, 2009. Frame, Framing, Framer, Framework, Framehouse.

29 Nick Schwartz, "Michael Jordan on Dean Smith: 'He was my mentor, my teacher, my second father'," *USAToday.com*, February 8, 2015, http://ftw.usatoday.com/2015/02/michael-jordan-remembers-dean-smith.

30 Aimee Lewis, "From being paralyzed by shame to coaching Serena Williams," *CNN.com*, August 15, 2017, http://www.cnn.com/2017/07/11/tennis/patrick-mouratoglou-serena-williams-pregnancy-wimbledon/index.html.

31 Mike James, "Kareem Abdul-Jabbar memorializes the great John Wooden in 'Coach Wooden and Me'," *LATimes.com*, June 22, 2017, http://www.latimes.com/books/jacketcopy/la-ca-jc-kareem-coach-wooden-20170621-story.html.

32 Paul Kent, "Angelo Dundee and Muhammad Ali shared an unbreakable bond," *DailyTelegraph.com*, February 2, 2012, http://www.dailytelegraph.com.au/sport/boxing-mma/angelo-dundee-and-muhammad-ali-shared-an-unbreakable-bond/news-story/1580aca53d71e55a7a2b313cd1499767?sv=9da7e2ee1e04e6e0deac77c3dd3ced6e.

33 Rachel Nuwer, "Coaching Can Make or Break an Olympic Athlete," *ScientificAmerican.com*, August 5, 2016, https://www.scientificamerican.com/article/coaching-can-make-or-break-an-olympic-athlete/.

34 Ibid.

35 Michael Anthony, "Don't Be a Donald This Christmas," *Townhall.com*, December 9, 2016, https://townhall.com/columnists/michaelanthony/2016/12/09/dont-be-a-donald-this-christmas-n2257152.

36 Screen capture, "CNN Interview with Michael Anthony, Godfactor.com Founder," YouTube.com, June 30, 2016, https://www.youtube.com/watch?v=5EeMfbIB3H8

37 "Steven Seagal Interview," *AikiWeb.com*, June 15, 2005, http://www.aikiweb.com/forums/showthread.php?t=8343.

38 Best MMA, "Steven Seagal finally reveals truths about Aikido," *YouTube.com*, September 14, 2016, https://www.youtube.com/watch?v=35vcZ2DctLg.

39 Adam Kilgore, "The Packers should tank," *WashingtonPost.com*, November 7, 2017, https://www.washingtonpost.com/news/sports/wp/2017/11/07/the-packers-should-tank/?tid=a_inl&utm_term=.5358538a22b8.

40 Brad Kullman, "Take it from a former GM: We should not reward tanking. Here's a proposal to end it for good," *WashingtonPost.com*, November 14, 2017, https://www.washingtonpost.com/news/sports/wp/2017/11/14/take-it-from-a-former-gm-we-should-not-reward-tanking-heres-a-proposal-to-end-it-for-good/?utm_term=.dc10c295cbe8.

41 Ibid.

42 Stephanie Mencimer, "GOP Hipster Makeover?", *MotherJones.com*, January/February 2010, http://www.motherjones.com/politics/2010/01/gop-hipster-makeover/.

43 Ibid.

44 Tom Krattenmaker, *The Evangelicals You Don't Know: Introducing the Next Generation of Christians*, (New York: Rowman & Littlefield Publishers, 2013), 184.

45 Sarah Padbury, "Concert haul," WorldMag.com, July 6, 2012, https://world.wng.org/2012/07/concert_haul

46 Corey Moss, "Janet Jackson Issues Video Apology for Super Bowl Incident," *MTV.com*, February 3, 2004, http://www.mtv.com/news/1484801/janet-jackson-issues-video-apology-for-super-bowl-incident/.

47 Bob Unruh, "Dobson Says 'No Way' to McCain Candidacy," *WND.com*, January 13, 2007, http://www.wnd.com/2007/01/39667/.

48 Ruby Rich, "An Interview with Darren Aronofsky," Aronofsky.net, undated, http://aronofksy.tripod.com/interview20.html.

49 Greg Hartman, "Obsessing Over Hollywood's Racial Diversity," *LifeZette.com*, August 23, 2016, https://www.lifezette.com/popzette/obsessing-over-hollywoods-racial-diversity/.

50 Brian Godawa, "Darren Aronofsky's Noah: Environmentalist Wacko," *Godawa.com* (blog), October 29, 2012, http://godawa.com/darren-aronofskys-noah-environmentalist-wacko/.

51 " 'Noah' Film Receives Praise From Christian Evangelicals Unfazed By 'Creative Interpretation'," NHCLC.org, undated, https://nhclc.org/noah-

film-receives-praise-from-christian-evangelicals-unfazed-by-creative-interpretation/

52 Phil Cooke, "Why I'm Recommending Christians See the Movie 'Noah'," *PhilCooke.com*, undated, http://www.philcooke.com/christians-should-see-noah/.

53 Craig Detweiler, " 'Noah' Prompted a Flood of Faith Conversations," *ChristianityEveryday.com*, undated, https://www.christianityeveryday.com/index.php/noah-prompted-a-flood-of-faith-conversations/.

54 Ibid.

55 "Wait No More," *ICareAboutOrphans.org*, undated, http://icareaboutorphans.org/whatwedo/waitnomore/.

56 "Focus on the Family - CS Indy Partner to Support Foster Families," *KKTV.com*, May 9, 2011, http://www.kktv.com/home/headlines/Focus_on_the_Family_-_CS_Indy_Partner_to_Support_Foster_Families_121547674.html?site=mobile.

57 Electa Draper, "Focus buys Super Bowl spot featuring Tim Tebow," *DenverPost.com*. January 15, 2010, http://www.denverpost.com/2010/01/15/focus-buys-super-bowl-spot-featuring-tim-tebow/.

58 Frances Kissling and Kate Michelman, "What Tim Tebow's Super Bowl ad can teach the pro-choice movement," *WashingtonPost.com*, January 31, 2010, http://www.washingtonpost.com/wp-dyn/content/article/2010/01/29/AR2010012902505.html.

59 Editorial Board, "Super Bowl Censorship," *NYTimes.com*, January 30, 2010, http://www.nytimes.com/2010/01/31/opinion/31sun4.html.

60 Richard Huff, "Super Bowl ratings: Saints victory over Colts was most-watched program of all time, beating 'MASH'," *NYDailyNews.com*, February 8, 2010, http://www.nydailynews.com/entertainment/tv-movies/super-bowl-ratings-saints-victory-colts-most-watched-program-time-beating-mash-article-1.194592.

61 "Super Bowl Ad Research: New Barna Study Examines Tebow/Focus Commercial," *Barna.com*, February 15, 2010, https://www.barna.com/research/super-bowl-ad-research-new-barna-study-examines-tebowfocus-commercial/.

62 Ibid.

63 Speeches by President Kennedy at United Negro College Fund fundraiser, Indianapolis, Indiana, April 12, 1959; and Valley Forge Country Club, Valley Forge, Pennsylvania, October 29, 1960.

64 Lisa Buckingham and Frank Kane, "Gerald Ratner's 'crap' comment haunts jewellery chain," *The Guardian.com*, August 22, 2014, https://www.

theguardian.com/business/2014/aug/22/gerald-ratner-jewellery-total-crap-1992-archive.

65 Reuters staff, "BP CEO apologizes for 'thoughtless' oil spill comment," Reuters.com, June 2, 2010, https://www.reuters.com/article/us-oil-spill-bp-apology/bp-ceo-apologizes-for-thoughtless-oil-spill-comment-idUSTRE6515NQ20100602.

66 Dan Merica and Elizabeth Landers, "Spicer apologizes for Hitler comparison: 'It was a mistake to do that'," *CNN.com*, April 12, 2017, http://www.cnn.com/2017/04/11/politics/sean-spicer-hitler-assad-gas-chemical-weapons/index.html.

67 Hannah Waldram, "#Susanalbumparty: Top five Twitter hashtag PR disasters," *TheGuardian.com*, November 22, 2012, https://www.theguardian.com/technology/shortcuts/2012/nov/22/twitter-susan-boyle-susanalbumparty.

68 Daniel Gaitan, "Tribute Island draws large, enthusiastic crowd to Kenosha's lakefront," *KenoshaNews.com*, July 23, 2017, http://www.kenoshanews.com/news/local/tribute-island-draws-large-enthusiastic-crowd-to-kenosha-s-lakefront/article_9eebad68-3502-5475-afdc-976edaf1c1f4.html.

69 Ibid.

70 Dan Gilgoff, "Evangelical Leader Dobson Doesn't Like Fred Thompson," *U.S. News & World Report* via *CBSNews.com*, March 28, 2007, https://www.cbsnews.com/news/evangelical-leader-dobson-doesnt-like-fred-thompson/.

71 Ibid.

72 "Dobson: I Didn't Disparage Fred Thompson's Faith." *WND.com*, March 30, 2017, http://www.wnd.com/2007/03/40876/.

73 Ibid.

74 Gary Schneeberger, "Dobson didn't propose a third political party," *DenverPost.com*, October 30, 2007, http://blogs.denverpost.com/opinion/2007/10/30/dobson-didn%E2%80%99t-propose-a-third-political-party/736/.

75 Ibid.

76 Chloe Melas, "Louis C.K.: 'These stories are true'," *CNN.com*, November 10, 2017, http://www.cnn.com/2017/11/10/entertainment/louis-ck-apology/index.html.

77 Glenn Beck, Twitter post, March 16, 2013, 7:52 p.m. ET, https://twitter.com/glennbeck/status/313120671297306624.

78 Photo from Paul Bond, " 'Bible' Producers Cut Satan Scenes From 'Son of God' Following Obama Controversy (Video.)" *HollywoodReporter.com*, February 17, 2014, https://www.hollywoodreporter.com/news/bible-producers-cut-satan-scenes-680781.

79 Mark Burnett, Twitter post, March 5, 2013, 4:01 p.m. PT, https://twitter.com/markburnetttv/status/309091262651310081.

80 Jordan Zakarin, "In History's 'The Bible,' Satan Looks Like President Obama (Photo)," *HollywoodReporter.com*, March 18, 2013, https://www.hollywoodreporter.com/live-feed/bible-satan-obama-lookalikes-photo-429343.

81 Ibid.

82 Roma Downey, "Producer: Why we cast 'Obama' devil out of 'Son of God'," *USAToday.com*, February 17, 2014, https://www.usatoday.com/story/opinion/2014/02/17/television-god-devil-obama-movie-roma-downey-column/5560379/.

83 Mike Huckabee, Daily Bread endorsement, *RWPVideo.org*, undated, https://www.rwpvideo.org/.

84 Mike Parker, "A Conversation With Producer Nina May," *BuddyHollywood.com*, November 2, 2017, http://buddyhollywood.com/a-conversation-with-producer-nina-may/.

85 Steve Jordahl, " 'Daily Bread' a daily dose of anti-Hollywood," *OneNewsNow.com*, November 3, 2017, https://www.onenewsnow.com/media/2017/11/03/daily-bread-a-daily-dose-of-anti-hollywood.

About the Author

Gary Schneeberger's three decades in journalism and public relations fuel his passion for, and success in, strategic marketing and communications.

As founder and president of ROAR, Schneeberger draws on his executive and executional experience in entertainment, ministry and media to help individuals and organizations engage audiences with the boldness and creative clarity that ensures they are heard. The ROAR team has earned clients coverage in hundreds of local and regional news outlets, plus national platforms from *The New York Times* to *USA Today*, *Time* to *Sports Illustrated*, NPR to the BBC, and every major broadcast and cable TV network in your channel lineup.

He has advised Hollywood studios (Universal, Warner Bros., 20th Century Fox), television networks (USA, History, The CW), global ministries (Focus on the Family), and publishing houses (Simon & Schuster.) He has counseled and created communications platforms for authors, experts, speakers, coaches and consultants of every conceivable stripe, from some of the biggest names in movies and TV to true mom-and-pop shops.

He has an extensive background as a spokesperson, appearing on the *CBS Evening News*, *CNN This Morning*, NPR and HLN, among scores of others.

Schneeberger also spent more than 15 years as an award-winning reporter and editor for newspapers coast-to-coast, including the *Los Angeles Times*.

He and his wife, Kelly, live in Camp Lake, Wisconsin, with her children, Alyssa and Hunter.

Bite the Dog is his first book.